T0146622

God instructs us to give our whole life to him as a holy and living sacrifice. But how do we do this? What does it mean to truly surrender your life to God as a sacrifice? One great way is to pattern yourself after Israel's offerings.

Give *Your All* to God focuses on the burnt offering and explains how while the people of Israel used a physical animal as a sacrifice, today we offer every part of our lives to God. And just as the physical offering was divided into five parts and burned up completely, we can take this unique example and apply it to our own sacrifice of our heart, soul, strength, mind, and everything else. Author Morris Williams presents sixteen worship behaviors that we can offer to God every day, enabling us to be a complete and total offering to God.

You must give your all to God, and doing so is what pleases him as you follow his instructions. And likewise, surrendering fully to God is part of his plan of salvation through Jesus Christ—the ultimate sacrifice, who died for you so you could become a valued member of God's family.

Give Your All
to
GOD

"… Williams [shows] with …enthusiasm the many ways we can " give our all " to the Creator, to our fellowman beings, and to Jesus, who gave his all to us. He delves deeply into what is meant by offering and sacrifice, translating those ideas into practical actions… all with the intention of motivating us to seek, find, and exalt God in every life situation…; to express compassion and help others; … showing that we can consistently devote ourselves to God. Williams' treatise is neatly organized with relevant references and could serve as a study focus for religious workshops."

U.S. Review of Book   by Barbara B. Scott

Give Your All to GOD

Be a Pleasing and Delightful Offering

MORRIS WILLIAMS

iUniverse®

GIVE YOUR ALL TO GOD
BE A PLEASING AND DELIGHTFUL OFFERING

iUniverse books may be ordered through booksellers or by contacting:

iUniverse
1663 Liberty Drive
Bloomington, IN 47403
www.iuniverse.com
1-800-Authors (1-800-288-4677)

Because of the dynamic nature of the Internet, any web addresses or links contained in
this book may have changed since publication and may no longer be valid. The views
expressed in this work are solely those of the author and do not necessarily reflect the views
of the publisher, and the publisher hereby disclaims any responsibility for them.

Any people depicted in stock imagery provided by Getty Images are models,
and such images are being used for illustrative purposes only.
Certain stock imagery © Getty Images.

ISBN: 978-1-5320-6546-0 (sc)
ISBN: 978-1-5320-6589-7 (hc)
ISBN: 978-1-5320-6545-3 (e)

Library of Congress Control Number: 2019900311

Print information available on the last page.

iUniverse rev. date: 11/19/2019

CONTENTS

INTRODUCTION

I have taught infants to fifth graders for forty-seven years. I have seen a combination of regular students and resource students among six subjects. I spent the last eight years as a resource teacher serving children with mild disabilities. I received a bachelor's degree at Morgan State University. I received a master's degree at Towson State University. My Thirty-Plus credits were earned at Northwestern State University, Natchitoches, LA. I was an educational consultant at a parent-and-child center during the summer four times in Baltimore. Johns Hopkins Hospital was our grantee agency. I won Teacher of the Month teaching resource students two times. I taught undergraduate adults as an itinerant teacher for two years through Northwestern State University, Natchitoches, LA.

As a regular church member, I seek to serve as best I can. Beginning with putting up and taking down chairs, helping with the boys club, and praying for others. Singing on the choir was a great experience. I became the coordinator for Youth Sunday Church and activities for many years. Being a born-again Christian, I am dedicated to learning God's Word deeper. Putting those learning into my life-long desire. This book is the result of ten-plus years of diligent study and following God's instruction, counsel, and guidance. I was blessed to have outstanding authors, pastors, and preachers share their understanding. I seek to love God better, reflect Jesus better, and love others better.

Originally, God planned to teach Adam and Eve how to prepare for the Kingdom of God by living the way of love. God wanted to guide humankind toward living better as He prepared them to serve Him toward eternal life. The tree of life would be available.

What Brought About the Need for Jesus Christ to Die for Humankind?

Because of the rebellion of Lucifer (who became Satan) and other fallen angels, God knew that no being other than Himself could avoid sin. He wanted a being of holy righteous character to also restore the government on earth based on love. They would become children in His family. So He decided to truly make humanity in His image. Men and women would need the ability to think, to reason, to form attitudes, and to make decisions. But first, they would start out made of flesh and blood and composed of matter. They would be subject to eternal death without repentance, grace, and maturity. They would need help from God. They would become God beings showing God finished the first phase of reproducing Himself. This is His master plan, and it leads to His greatest purpose.

Before the foundation of the earth, God in His wisdom and understanding of humankind set up plan A, which was ready to execute to correct their distant relationship. The triune God was never caught off guard. He didn't have to come up with a plan B. He knew humankind would need deliverance from sin. Jesus Christ was ready, willing, and able to pay the ultimate price (John 6:37–40). This would enable people to reconcile themselves to the Holy God (Hebrews 9:14; 10:10–14). God knew that humankind would need the Son's redeeming atonement. The Word was prepared to lay aside His divine and righteous self-existence. He would be born of human flesh.

Sin entered when Adam and Eve disobeyed God (after the devil had deceived them). Beginning from Adam's time, humanity perverted and corrupted everything that God had given and also perverted the use of sacrifices (Deuteronomy 12:31–32). "They even burn their sons and daughters in the fire as sacrifices to their gods."

Sin had cut humanity off from God and the tree of life (the Spirit and truth of God). God wanted humanity and Israel to simply obey His voice and walk in all the ways He commanded them. He wanted them to bring justice and judgment. He wanted them to have broken and contrite hearts.

There had to be a blood sacrifice for the forgiveness of sin. God now required animal sacrifices to provide for the temporary forgiveness of sin. There is no remission of sin without the shedding of blood (Hebrews 9:22).

A *sacrifice* is defined as the offering up of something precious for a cause or a reason. Those who are covered by the blood sacrifice are set free from the consequences of sin—death. Animal sacrifices were commanded by God so that the individual could experience the forgiveness of sin. The animal served as a substitute—that is, the animal died in place of the sinner, but only temporarily, which is why the animal sacrifices needed to be offered over and over.

Jesus Christ's main purpose for coming to earth as a man was to die for humankind. He shed His precious innocent blood to meet the requirement the Father had set. He had to be accepted by the Father. Sins must be taken away and justified. This is the main reason the offering of bulls, lambs, and goats happened during the Old Testament times. It acted as a reminder. They would look forward to the time when the final sacrifice would be made—Jesus Christ, the Lamb of God. It is impossible for the blood of bulls and goats to take away sins (Hebrew 10:1–4).

The sacrifice of Jesus Christ would be the bridge that would connect the vast space between the holy God and earthy sinful humankind. There is no human way for the huge unpassable gap to be crossed. It would take The Word to make it possible for the differences to be bridged. Humankind would then be reconciled to God, receive His Holy Spirit, and become God's sons and daughters.

If Jesus Christ did not die for us, we would be doomed to eternal death. Life would not have any true purpose or meaning. We would just live and die without the hope of existing to or beyond seventy years. Living with God for eternity would be impossible. We would be doomed to eternal spiritual death.

But the Father and Jesus Christ had a plan and purpose for humankind. They knew humanity wouldn't keep the law. They knew the ultimate sacrifice would be needed. Jesus knew it would require Him giving up His godliness and divine existence temporally. He had to give up His glorified divine life and shed His blood as a perfect sinless person. He also knew Satan and humankind would make it very hard. He knew he would have to live a perfect sinless life as both God and man. He could not give in to temptations, trials, and wrong desires. The triune God decided it would be worth the effort for humankind to finally become part of the great eternal existence He enjoyed. God has always wanted to be in a very close relationship with humanity, whom He created in His image.

God planned for several events to better humankind. A lot of understanding, customs, and habits had to be changed, clarified, and even erased. There had to be a lot of preparation in order before Jesus got to earth. His appearance and character would have to be foretold by the right people at the right time. God did everything just right.

Above all, He would be the greatest final sacrifice needed to bridge the great gap between humankind and God. Jesus was the best member of the divine family to do this. He could go to earth as a human and be subjected to the pulls of human nature.

Sacrifices and offerings were made so that people could remember the sins that separated us from God (Isaiah 59:2), the need for repentance, and the need for an intercessor, Jesus Christ. He brings all this into focus.

We must always ask how sacrifices point to Jesus Christ. The law was meant to serve as a schoolmaster to bring us to repentance and lead us to Christ (Romans 7:7; Galatians 3:19–24). Jesus's blood was shed so that our sins could be passed over with the penalty paid in full. We are pardoned, forgiven, and reconciled to God when we accept His sacrifice and repent. Just like the bulls and goats, Jesus did no wrong. He willingly gave Himself and died in our place. "God the Father had Jesus, who had no sin to be sin for us, so that in him we might become the righteousness of God" (2 Corinthians 5:21).

Children of God and Heirs with Israel

Believers in Christ have been chosen for the same purpose as the nation of Israel. We are called to be holy and be blameless in God's sight (Exodus 19:6; 1 Peter 2:9). We are to reflect God's character to the world around us. We are to dedicate all parts of our lives to God. If you belong to Christ, you are Abraham's seed and heirs to the promises of eternal life (Galatians 3: 7-9,29). God would justify the Gentiles by faith. All nations shall be blessed with Abraham. God wants you to offer every part of yourself as an instrument of righteousness. This leads to holiness. This leads to eternal life. His plan is for you to be in the God family. He wants you to offer spiritual sacrifices to Him through Jesus Christ (Romans 12:1). Jesus is the connection between Israel and the children of God. That is why we are spiritual Israelites.

"This mystery is that through the gospel the Gentiles are heirs together with Israel, members together of one body, and sharers together in the promise in Christ Jesus" (Ephesians 3:6).

Types of Offerings

Every sacrifice that an Israelite offered was of a certain type and for a specific purpose. Every offering has very exacting rules as to what is offered, how it is offered, and by whom it is offered. For example, the peace offering could be eaten on the day it was sacrificed or on the day after but not on the third day. To eat this sacrificial meat on the third would have serious results (Leviticus 19:5–8). A burnt offering had to be male, while the peace offering could have been a male or a female animal but not a bird. Because of the consequences for failing to observe the laws of the offerings, people had to be certain what offering they were making and then make it in accordance with the laws of God.

First, the people would have to decide which offerings they were making and why. They had to decide which animals they would and could offer. Second, they would lay their hands on the heads of the animals. This action was a symbol of transferring to the animal their sinfulness. They had to own up to their sins. The animals took the place of the offerors and became their substitutes. Third, they had to kill the animals, which pointed out the necessity for death of the individuals whose sins alienated them from God. This showed these people wanted to be forgiven.

There are five types of offerings an Israelite would make—sin offering (Leviticus 4:1–35), trespass/guilt offering (Leviticus 7:1–9) burnt offering (Leviticus 1:1–17), meal/grain offering (Leviticus 2:1–16), and trespass/quilt offering (Leviticus 3:1–17). This is the order in which they are understood and apply to us as Jesus Christ fulfilled them. You will see that this order of offerings guides you through the process of being at one with God.

Thus, I will describe the offerings starting with the sin offering and move ahead to the trespass offering. This sequence outlined the spiritual importance of the sacrificial system. First, sin had to be dealt with—sacrifice of expiation (sin or trespass offerings). Then the worshippers could commit themselves completely to God—sacrifice of consecration (burnt offering and grain offering). Next, fellowship or communion between the Lord, the priest, and the worshippers was established—sacrifice of communion (peace offering). The offering of thanksgiving can be included with the peace offering if the offerors want. I'll discuss the thanksgiving offering in more detail in the section titled "Be Thankful to God and Your Neighbor."

God set up these offerings with the future in mind—Jesus Christ. Each offering helps you review what you need to do for a close relationship with God. It starts with repenting and asking for forgiveness. It ends with seeking a closer peace and fellowship with God Himself.

All the offerings served to constantly remind Israelites that God is totally holy. The system was designed by God with the intention of reminding us that sin separates us from God. The system shows us the possibility of obtaining the forgiveness of sin and becoming righteous before God through Jesus Christ.

Give a Total Offering to God—Yourself

The burnt offering is the major focus of this book. It must be viewed in context with other offerings. The sequence allows you to see the relationship each has with the others. There are two offerings before it and two after.

God wants us to dedicate ourselves to Him totally. He wants us to dedicate our minds, hearts, souls, and strength to Him first. God wants us to present ourselves as living sacrifices that are holy and acceptable to Him (Romans 12:1–3).

All the offerings point to Jesus Christ. This law of sacrifice and offerings was fulfilled by Jesus Christ for us (1 Corinthians 5:7).

Several prophets of God wanted the sacrifices to include faith, confession, and devotion. Isaiah contented that the sacrifices were worthless if the person didn't have repentance and lead an obedient life.

Micah reflected the same sentiments when he proclaimed that God was not interested in the physical act of sacrifice by itself but in the life and heart of the one making the sacrifice. Jeremiah pointed out that the symbol of the sacrifice must be reflected in the individual's life. Malachi chastised the people for offering the lame and sick animals to God instead of the best. Those who did this were defiling the altar and despising God. Hosea reflected God's true desire for mercy, not sacrifice, and acknowledgment of God rather than burnt offerings (Hosea 6:6). Truly, God wants us to offer our hearts and lives to Him completely.

This third offering Israel made to God was the burnt offering. It was a total body offering that was completely burned up on an altar. The bull or goat was cut into five groups—head, legs, innards, fat, and the rest of the body. Each reflected a different meaning. When considering the parts, you have the whole. The *head* showed the use of the mind, making decisions and having higher thoughts acceptable to God. The *legs* showed active participation and going in the direction of light and truth. But the *innards* of the sacrifice showed feelings, desires, and motivations toward our Lord's ways. Surely, God wants us to desire truth in the inner parts. Then the *fat* was burned too. This revealed the strength and health we needed as we sought to please God. The *rest of the body* also was burned up. We are constantly transforming our new lives to reflect God's ways. This represented our whole life, which we give to God.

This book further describes sixteen worship behaviors we can offer to God. These sacrifices are grouped into the five parts of the whole burnt offering mentioned previously. The character traits God wants to see in us are further developed. We benefit greatly when we give ourselves totally to God. We are to offer ourselves with our minds, the directions we go, and the motivation to do well, using our strengths to do well and be pleasing to Him. God wants us to use our minds, hearts, souls, and strength to worship Him. He wants all of you. He wants us to be total living sacrifices to Him. He wants us to dedicate our entire lives to Him. He wants to be involved in all parts of our lives, including the good times and the hard times.

The best way for us to prove that holiness even exists in our lives is to live it out in good relationships with others. We must care more about God than we do about ourselves. God wants us to love Him first and then love others.

The practice of holiness is for the strong hearted only. It is the day-to-day life of those who are filled with the presence of the Holy Spirit and who, by His power, are losing concern for themselves. Our love for Him is shown not only in our commitment to right living but also in our love for people. You will put God first, all others second, and yourself a distant third. Your life will be marked by love for others. Our relationship with others is important, including with those in authority over us. It includes how we face injustice and suffering. Remember the two commands of love—love God and love your neighbor.

God always wanted us to do right with our fellow man (Leviticus 19:11–18). He does want us doing what's right and just. See chapter 6, "Do What's Right and Just," in this book for suggestions.

You are to love your neighbor as yourself. To truly love involves love of God and love for your fellow man (Matthew 22:36–40). This pleases God greatly.

The goal of this book is to guide you so that you can focus on becoming that total sacrifice that is blemish-free.

Let us not forget that doing these offerings does not earn you salvation. It is God who offers us forgiveness and eternal life as a free gift in Jesus Christ. It is your love relationship with God that makes you so unique. Being forgiven of your sins and accepting the great sacrifice of Jesus keeps you on an awesome journey of being an ever-growing child of God. Making the various offerings shows that you actually love and cherish your relationship with Him. You accept the truth that Jesus has already done the work. You accept the truth that God created you for future service on earth and also service in eternity with God's family.

This book focuses on the burnt offering of freely and totally devoting your whole life to God. It was completely burned up on the altar. Jesus Christ is our altar. We are to completely be consumed with pleasing God as we worship Him. In addition, God wants you to give Him your very best. He doesn't want second best or something you half-heartedly give.

First, consider what areas you are strong or need more guidance in. Remember this is a total package. You should not seek to include a few areas and disregard others. Ask God to lead you in where to begin and areas you already devote to Him. You can use the sections as a prayer list. You give yourself to God in ways you don't recognize and realize. Since your mind really determines what you say and do, check where you are with the first area of the head. Use your mind to purposely focus on your relationship with God. Then your love for music and gospel songs will help you give praise, thanks, and honor to God. Some songs summarize your quest to give your best to God.

The greatest feature about God is that He is ready and willing to give you the help and support you'll need. All we have to do is ask and expect answers. His Word tells us that He is "compassionate and gracious, slow to anger, abounding in love and faithfulness, maintain love to thousands, and forgiving wickedness, rebellion and sin" (Exodus 34:6–7). Yet He does not leave the guilty unpunished. Ask Him to teach you His ways so you may know Him better and continue to find favor with Him (Exodus 33:13). God sees Christ's righteousness in you because of the blood He shed. So, actually, you are seeking to become more like Jesus Christ. The Holy Spirit gives us power to change however we need to.

With Jesus and the new covenant, physical sacrifices are no longer required. True repentance and confession enables God to forgive us. Prayers and a dedicated life have taken the place of animal sacrifices. God expects you to keep giving your very best.

CHAPTER ONE

Repent of Sin Toward God

Sin Offering

The sin offering was the very first of the five offerings the Israelite made to God (Leviticus 4). It was the most important step toward being reconciled to God. This refers to the confession of all we think, say, or do that displeases God. Of course, the commandments were already given to them. It was an offering to atone for and purge a sin. To atone is to make the relationship right when it is broken because of our sins. It was an expression of sorrow for the error committed through carelessness, ignorance, rushing, or a lack of consideration. The person wanted to be forgiven of sin. Sin occurs because of our carnal human nature, human weaknesses, and our evil tendencies.

All people knew they needed forgiveness and a way to make everything right with God. We would be hopeless without that possibility of improving our relationship with God. They knew they fell short of His glory. There is a missing desire or a void (emptiness) when they don't have a close relationship with God. Until that offering is made, people are usually very

1

concerned and worried about the offense against the commands of God. They knew things were not going to get any better until they confessed and were forgiven. They knew that without the shedding of blood, there was no forgiveness of sin.

God knew that people would sin. So He set up a sacrificial system that used animals to help them deal with sin. He knew Jesus Christ would need to come to earth to make the final sacrifice for the sins of humankind. We would then be reconciled to Him. God knew humanity would fall short.

The sin offering was of no avail when the person showed purposeful rebellion against God.

In the Old Testament, people atoned symbolically for their sins by offering animal sacrifices to God. Israel knew something was going to happen in the future to complete this process of sacrifice. In the New Testament, Jesus Christ is our sin offering. He has given humanity a chance to repent and become acceptable to God (2 Peter 3:9). By our acts of repentance and confessing our sins, we offer our sins to God, seeking His forgiveness.

Israel desired to offer a sacrifice because they knew they needed forgiveness and a way to make everything right with God.

During Old Testament times, the type of sacrifice made depended on who committed the unintentional sin and the financial ability of the person. The priest or the congregation had to offer a bull. A leader of the people offered a male goat. The regular or common people offered a female goat or lamb. The poor could usually only offer two young turtledoves. In the case of extreme poverty, family could substitute fine flour as a sacrifice. Believers today just pray to God for forgiveness.

The animal could have no defects. God would not accept the sacrifice if there were any blemishes on it. In the New Testament, Jesus corrected the relationship between God and humanity once and for all by dying for our sins. He was resurrected. He was a perfect offering. He was a perfect sinless offering. He was without blemishes or defects in character. He was without the blemishes discussed in the trespass offering/quilt offering.

This book focuses on the common and regular sinner who is able to pray to Father God at any time.

Procedure of Offering

The offerors would lay their hands on the animals that were the sin offerings. They would slaughter these creatures at the place of burnt offerings. Laying hands on the animal showed that their sins were transferred to the animals (Leviticus 4:4). They would slaughter the animal at the place of the burnt offerings. The sinners showed recognition of sins in themselves and the willingness to lay down their sinful lives. Then the priest would place some of the blood on the horn of the altar of the burnt offerings. The priest then poured the rest of the blood at the base of the altar. All the fatty portions (fat covering inner parts, fat tail, kidneys, and a lobe of the liver) would be removed and burned on the altar. This was God's portion. These offerors had no portion. The priest would present the offering as atonement for the offerors' sins to the Lord. They would be forgiven. All remaining meat had to be eaten by a male in the priest's family within the tabernacle—in the holy place (Leviticus 6:26).

The burning of the fat was a sweet savor to God. This symbolically reflected the person handing over the better part of humanity to God. We all sin and come short of the glory of God. It doesn't matter if we are rich or poor, a leader or a minister. We still sin and deserve death. Confess your sin to God.

The sin offering also reminds us of the consequences of sin (death) and the need for a Savior. The sin offering also reveals how much God hates our sins (Romans 8:3). Sin separates us from God. God wants us to turn from our wicked ways by becoming a new creature seeking to live His way.

No matter how offensive or grave our sins are, God is willing to forgive us. However, He will not forgive anyone speaking against the Holy Spirit. His will is that all would repent and come to the glory of God. Unrepentant sin leads to eternal death.

"For what the law was powerless to do because it was weakened by the flesh, God did by sending his own Son in the likeness of sinful flesh to be a sin offering" (Romans 8:3).

Jesus Christ is our sin offering.

Jesus-Connected

Jesus is the only way our sins will be forgiven. He is the only way to achieve a close relationship with God our Father. He is the way to eternal life. He is the answer to everything we need. Look at the appendix 1 to learn about the many reasons Jesus should be the center of your life.

You are connected to Jesus Christ already as your personal Savior, creator, judge, friend, King of Kings, and master builder for starters. He is already set to be and do these outstanding favors for you. He is all of these and so much more. All you have to do is claim that connection. He is positioned to become these to you personally right now. All you have to do is recognize you have access to His unlimited and awesome resources. Jesus is prepared to do everything that really matters for you and with you. All you have to do is ask and believe. You are destined for greatness and have a future you can't imagine.

You get connected to an unfailing combination and relationship. Thank them for being available. When you get connected to Jesus, you are connected to the awesome love of Father God and the intimate inspiration of Holy Spirit. When you worship God by being fruitful, you have a vital connection to Jesus. "Everything we do can be an act of worship."

All we have to do is confess our sins to Jesus Christ and accept His loving sacrifice. Your sins are then forgiven. Get baptized. The Holy Spirit will further teach you about Jesus Christ. He will encourage you to read the Word. Then ask Him to guide you so that you can become a faithful Christian for the rest of your life. Ask Him to give you the zeal to keep learning and doing God's will. Ask God to guide you so that you can become more like Jesus Christ through the Holy Spirit (John 14:26 NKJV).

Jesus is always preparing us for more responsibility, working on our behalf, and getting us to bear more fruit. This is the person we should want to know better.

Jesus is able to do it all. He should be everything to you. He is the center of our salvation. Because Jesus shed His blood for us and was resurrected, you have the hope of eternal life. We can be forgiven of our sins. We can confidently attack problems, knowing He is with us, for us, and in us. The fight is fixed. We will win the war. He is our source of peace and joy. We know He has conquered death. He is our all.

So no matter what sin you commit (except against the Holy Spirit), God will forgive you. You must take the steps to ask for forgiveness and accept Jesus's sacrifice. In the model prayer by Jesus, He tell us to confess our sins to God. He expects this to be done daily.

Our salvation began with the true love of God when He sent His only Son to die for our penalty of death. He also destroyed the works of the devil. You get to know the Father only because you know Jesus. Whoever has the Son has the Father (John 14:10–15 NLT). You get to know Holy Spirit only because you know Jesus Christ (John 15:26; Romans 8:26–27 NLT).

Jesus is the source of true hope. You would be hopeless without the possibility of deepening your relationship with God through Jesus. There is a deep void when we don't have a close relationship with God. How close you are to God, how much you know God, how deeply you love God, and how strongly you obey God depend on you. He is our source of satisfaction, confidence, peace, and eternal life.

The full meaning of the sin offering represented what was required of our Savior to fulfill the penalty for our disobedience. This offering was needed to redeem us from eternal death. We all earned the penalty because of our worldly works. Jesus Christ had to fulfill the requirements for us since we could not redeem ourselves from the corruption of sin (Romans 5:6–11 NLT). This is an incredible gift.

The sin offering is not just about forgiveness and Jesus taking the penalty for us. It is also about fulfilling the desire to have a deeper relationship with God. It is about filling that void so that you can know God better. Nothing can separate us from the love of Jesus. It's about humbling yourself to Jesus. Then God can build you up and enrich you. The sin offering also helps us recognize that Jesus is the answer to everything we want and need. Finally, we should realize how deep, wide, and high the love of Jesus has for you is. No one and nothing can take away the love He has for you. God wants you to have an abundant life with confidence.

Jesus—Our Passover and Communion

Despite of the nine plagues God sent on Egypt to free Israel from slavery, He gave the tenth plague of the firstborn. Every firstborn of cattle and humanity would die (Exodus 12:13 NKJV).

But God gave the Israelites instructions to sacrifice a lamb and put the blood on their doorposts. Then the death angel passed over whoever had this blood on the doorpost. Unleavened bread and spices were also eaten with the Passover lamb. They were waiting for word about when they could leave Egypt.

This was a sign and a symbol about the coming of Jesus Christ. Israel and you were redeemed with the precious blood of Jesus as the lamb. It must be without a blemish and without spots.

In God's eyes, we have been slaves of sin just as the Israelites were slaves to Pharaoh. God's plan is to set us free. We must be willing to submit to His rule. Since we all have sinned, we must pay the penalty of death. But "God so loved the world that He gave His only begotten Son" to bear the sins of many (John 3:16). Jesus paid the death penalty for us.

Many Jews of the old covenant (Old Testament) observed this as a holy day until Jesus changed the symbols. The Feast of Unleavened Bread was also observed. Go to section 16, "Be a Priest for the Gospel" to further understand the part Jesus has in the eight festivals of Israel.

Remember Jesus introduced the New Testament symbols just before He was crucified. At the Last Supper, Jesus poured water into a basin and began to wash the disciples' feet. He dried their feet with a towel. This is a lesson in humility and service to others (Philippians 2:3, 5).

Then Jesus passed out a loaf of unleavened bread. Jesus said this represented His body. He voluntarily gave Himself to be beaten and to die for us. He is the perfect sinless sacrifice that was offered. He suffered so He might take our infirmities and bear our sickness (Isaiah 53:3–5) as our healer. Bread is also associated with life. Jesus is the bread that makes eternal life possible for us. He wants us to be justified and then reconciled to Father God.

Next, Jesus gave the disciples wine to drink. Jesus said, "This is my blood of the new covenant, which is shed for many for the remission of sin. This sacrifice made the forgiveness of sin and removal of our guilt possible. This opened the way for the new covenant. God make the covenant with believers by writing His laws on our hearts and minds.

"The Passover is a present picture of living the fulfilled life. It is a constant reminder that we are no longer slaves in the bondage of sin because Messiah our Passover has been sacrificed. We are now free to follow and honor the Lord, and to live as new creatures through Messiah's gracious atonement."[1]

Taking communion regularly is the continual sign of the new covenant that Jesus began. We remember what Jesus went through just for us. He shed His blood, and He allowed men to badly beat His body.

Jesus was the only person who could be offered for our sins. That's why He is our sin offering.

"Therefore, I urge you, brothers, in view of God's mercy, to offer your bodies as living sacrifices, holy and pleasing to God—this is your spiritual act of worship" (Romans 12:1).

---

[1] Sam Nadler, *Messiah in the Feasts of Israel*. Word of Messiah Ministries, Charlotte, NC. 2010, 57.

CHAPTER TWO

Fix Wrongs Against Others

Trespass Offering / Guilt Offering

Every offering was ordained to aid humanity's understanding of salvation (John 3:16–17).

The primary purpose of offerings is to draw close to God. This includes three features about offerings. The first feature is giving. The person is giving up something that belongs to him. Thus, you needed to have domestic animals. A second feature about offerings is to substitute. The animal being offered is a substitution for the person making the offering, and the things that are being done to the animal are the things that should have been done to the person. The third feature about offerings is coming close to God.

The true purposes of prayer are similar to those of sacrifices and offerings. We bring praise to God. We become closer to God and express love, thanks, or gratitude for atonement.

A part of God's plan in starting the five offerings was to teach people to hate sin and deter them from committing sin. The trespass offering does this.

The sacrificial system taught people the necessity of dealing with sin and at the same time demonstrated that God had provided a way to deal with that sin.

This foreshadows the fact that Christ is also our trespass offering and trespass (Colossians 2:13 NASB). The sin offering is first. It was sin made against God, and we atoned for our sins. After you are forgiven for your sin, you have salvation. The trespass offering is second because it is part of the sin offering. It atones for our offenses, faults, or trespasses toward one another after salvation. It was made against people, their property, or holy things. Forgetting to pay tithes would be an offense against holy things. The sin and trespass offerings were offered before the burnt offering, meal offering, and peace offering. These two are the mandatory offerings and sacrifices of expiation dealing with sin. While the next two (burnt and grain) were sacrifices of consecration, offerings are voluntary. These dealt with the worshipper committing him or herself completely to God. Lastly, the peace offering was a sacrifice of communion. Here a fellowship or communion was developed between the Lord, the priest, and the worshipper. A drink offering (wine) went along with this meal offering. Jesus told a man to be reconciled with his brother before he made his gift (burnt, meal, and peace) offering to God (Matthew 5:23–24 NJKV). Cain offered a freewill meal (the fruit of the ground) to cover his sin instead of the compulsory sin offering like Abel. God rejected this offer from Cain (Genesis 4:1–4; Hebrews 11:4).

Now let's look at what the trespass offering involves. With the trespass offering, if you have done anything that has caused injury to another person, you should make all reparation and make restitution where necessary. These consequences are often unintentional. The trespass sin happens when the person steps or slips over the mark, that line between right or wrong.

Procedure of Offering

The physical offering consisted of an animal, generally a ram. The ram was to be without blemishes. The very poor person might bring some fine flour. The animal was slain and burned on the altar. The blood was poured out at the altar. The ram's fatty portions (fat covering the inner parts, fat tail, kidneys, and a lobe of the liver) were burnt on the altar of burnt offerings for God (Leviticus 7:3–5 NLT). The remainder (meat) was to eaten in a holy place (court or tabernacle) by the priest. The offender got none of the meat. The officiating priest got the skin and any meat. However, any portions mixed in oil or those that were dried were divided among all the priests. The grain mixed in oil went toward the grain/meal offering. Only the priests could offer the trespass offering or any other sacrifice. The sinner actually killed the animal. The offering required sacrifice and the shedding of blood. The trespass offering was consumed by fire. Let the Word of God by the Holy Spirit purge you, test you, and prove you. Then you see what sort of work it is (1 Corinthians 3:13–15).

God gives ten examples of trespasses that must be fixed when you have wronged your neighbor (Leviticus 5:1–4, 15–17; 6:2–4 NLT). These also apply to us today. Paul reminds you not to wrong your brother or take advantage of him (1 Thessalonians 4:6–7 NKJV). The examples include the following: sin of silence, sin of defilement, swearing rashly, sin of dishonesty, sin of ignorance, failure in trust, sin in partnership, taking by violence, sin of deception, and sin of keeping things found.

1. *When you don't speak up or when you actually withhold evidence when it's necessary for justice, you have aided and abetted and become partner in the crime.* Achan brought spoils into the camp instead of dedicating them to God after defeating those at Jericho. The family didn't report this to Joshua. Thus, they were killed along with Achan (Joshua 7). When you see others commit crimes or serious wrongdoing, tell the authorities. You can do this secretly. *Otherwise, this is the sin of silence.*
2. If Israelites touched anything unclean (wild animals, livestock, or creatures) or interacted with human uncleanness, they were

considered unclean. Even if you didn't know about the situation, when you learned about it, you became unclean and guilty. This protected the community of contagious diseases. *Likewise, we need to take care in what we allow in our hearts, minds, and eyes. So when we see something unclean, wrong, or unwholesome, even if by accident, we must be cleansed.* Ask for God's help so that this exposure won't wrongly affect family, friends, and community members. Prejudice, jealously, high-mindedness, hatred, and bigotry are attitudes to look out for. These can infest you. *This the sin of defilement.*

3. The emphasis is on making an oath. *So we must be very careful what we say lest it leads us to sin. Being* humble and gentle is the safer way in life. Let your yes be yes and your no be no. Don't add oaths or promises you can't keep. God binds the person who binds him or herself by an oath (Matthew 5:33–37). So don't make an oath or promise you can't keep. *Don't swear rashly.*

4. You are being dishonest by withholding your tithes and offerings to your local church. God is robbed when we neglect time in church and time in the Word of God. *Be honest in holy things (time, possessions, abilities, activities, privileges, and friends).* This dishonesty in holy things is a trespass for which God requires amends and restoration. *Give yourself to your chosen church consistently. This is a sin of dishonesty.*

5. Man reasons that if he is ignorant, he can't be held responsible. Most of what we claim to be ignorant of is willful and therefore is sin. Our maker has a manual of what is acceptable conduct and rules to guide relationships with other people. This manual is the Holy Bible. Be humble and willing to learn what God expects of us. *If a person finds out but does not do it, he or she is guilty. Carelessness or needless forgetfulness is also a sin.* You pretend you don't know. *This is the sin of ignorance.*

6. *If you accept the property of another to hold, look after, or keep safe, you must do what you promised.* Someone has trusted you to be responsible and to return the item in the same condition as given. Also, when someone shares information in confidence with you, keep it to yourself. Do not be careless about something you are

expected to keep safe and quiet. The lie is not keeping the item or information safe. *This is failure in trust.*

7. *Doing your fair share is important everywhere.* Don't act as top dog, and take the easiest or glamorous jobs for yourself, leaving the dirty or mundane tasks for others. The lie is not playing fair. *This is the sin of partnership.*

8. *When you want your way without considering whether the conscience of others is hurt or offended, you take the mind or personality of others from them by violence.* The lie is that it is all right to abuse your authority and that you can even justify it. Respect others' rights and privileges. Bullying is not acceptable. *This is taking by violence.*

9. *The sin of deception means to obtain under false pretenses.* People try to run scams on others to get their money, possessions, power, or reputations. Employees deceive employers by trying to get recognition or credit for something they didn't do. Others embellish the facts to make things sound more attractive or their part greater. Some even try to deceive God. People try to scam others.

10. *When you find something, do your very best to find the true owner, and see that it is returned.* The lie is pretending you are the owner. God requires you to always be honest. *This is the sin of keeping things.*

Be aware of these so you can handle each rightly. All these small matters can prepare you for bigger things as you do good works with your fellow man.

These ten examples of trespasses seem small and even unimportant, but God mentioned them for a reason. Our life journey can be hindered or our direction changed because of a small step we didn't take with care properly. If you have a difficulty with your brother, fix it first. Then you can go to the altar of Jesus. Even though restitution was the main thing, there must be atonement for your sin against God. Matthew 5:23–24 (The Message) shows that restitution came before going to the altar. Our communion is broken with God until we make restitutions. Get it right with your fellow man first. Why not add a gift by way of compensation? Apologize. Ask for forgiveness. Treat your neighbor right.

God will not accept your prayer until you forgive or seek forgiveness from that person. God wants you to forgive others of their trespasses against you if you want forgiveness from God (Matthew 6:14–15).

Sometimes a person would commit an unknown sin. You may think you have trespassed against someone. It is possible that it did not really happen. Therefore, you make a voluntary offering. No restitution is involved.

This offering was placed on the altar. The altar points to Jesus Christ. This is where blood was shed to provide atonement. Under the new covenant, God recognizes Jesus Christ as the altar. Make sure you are going to Christ and no one else when you have problems.

All the meat offerings of animals could have no blemishes. Offerings could be rejected. They must be perfect to be accepted. This is true for any animal offering made to God. God requires sacrifices without these blemishes—blindness, broken, maimed, having a wen, scurvy, scabbed, no superfluous thing, bruised, crushed, broken, or cut. You rob God with any of these (Leviticus 22:20–22, 24). Likewise, all our spiritual offerings must be free of blemishes. These ten blemishes would better be placed with the sin offering. Jesus Christ became that perfect blameless sacrifice. Let's take a brief look at each act that can prevent you from being a perfect offering.

1. *Blindness shows a lack of understanding the Word of God.* If you try to move closer to God through philosophy (being honest as in Ephesians 1:18), vain deceit (deluded by the so-called wisdom of humankind as in James 4:13–18), the traditions of the world (the traditions that make the Word of God ineffective as in Mark 7:13), and the rudiments of the world (the lust of the flesh, lust of the eyes, pride of life is of this world as in 1 John 2:15–17), you are not after Christ. You are offering a blemished offering. You are robbing God!

2. *A broken offering shows unfaithfulness in your life toward to God (Ephesians 5:26–27). God expects you to stay with Him no matter what you are going through.* He is faithful to you. You are to be

faithful to Him. Stay with God no matter what. Give Him the credit for your success.

3. *Giving a maimed offering "deprives you of capacity for service or of strength, efficiency, or wholeness" (Leviticus 22:22–23). This means you are not at your best.* Nor are you giving others your very best. You are just trying to get by and get a check. You are just there, and you appear to be supporting the effort. But you aren't actually putting in the time and effort. God doesn't accept this half effort.

4. *A disfigured, mutilated, or wounded offering shows that you are corrupting the Word and turning the grace of God into a license for immorality (Jude 1:4).* You think God won't mind since He will forgive you anyway. Don't keep going your wrong way. You are not at your best.

5. *If there are scratches or skin diseases on the animal, you do not endure sound doctrine.* You want to hear the doctrines of humans that please the flesh (2 Timothy 4:3–4). You only want to hear your view and not talk about sin. *You should try to seek the truth.*

6. *If there are scratches, you are allowing yourself to be infected by the popular opinion, trends, and fads that infect the church world rather than abiding by the principles and patterns of the Word of God (1 Samuel 15:24; 16:7).* The Word of God must be your source of truth. The Bible should be your looking glass through which you view life.

7. *Superfluous things show deformity from being excessive in your life as you walk before the Lord. God wants you to be moderate and mild.* This includes your excessive eating and drinking, buying too many clothes and cars, and pursuing too much power and influence. This gives you a better than others attitude. Rather God wants you to stay humble.

8. *Here are three activities that show a misuse, misapplying, or wrongly focusing on scriptures in how you to relate to fellow Christians as well as those who don't know God.* You may tell others that the King James Version is the only Bible that people should use. You may tell others that only ordained ministers can minister to others by service. You may tell others that only your specific beliefs and traditions are correct. So don't judge others who have

less understanding of God than you. None of these character flaws will be accepted by God. You rob God of getting the best from you.

We have to resist the urge to give our worn-out old things to God while we keep what is new and best for ourselves. This includes our money, time, talents, zeal, love, dedication, and strength. God wants us to use these to serve Him and our fellow man with our best effort. This truly glorifies God.

There is an order of action God expects when you trespass against another person. First, make restitution to the offended or injured person if needed. Second, give recompense if necessary. Third, remember that the sacrifice was given as atonement for the sin. Depending on the person's ability to pay, he would give a ram, two doves or pigeons, or fine flour. The injured person must be paid for the wrongdoing. Christians today are to fix the wrong they did to God or their neighbors. Apologize.

You also are to present yourself to Father God without any blemishes. Through His death, Jesus can present you holy and without blemishes (Colossians 1:22). He presents the radiant church to Himself without stain or wrinkles or any other blemish but rather holy and blameless (Ephesians 5:27 NLT).

"By our trespass, we have sinned and forfeited our life. The sacrifice of Jesus as a trespass offering has bought and paid for our life and fulfilled our debts." "When we wrong or offend others, we can ask Christ to make intercession for us with them. When we have done our part Christ will restore us. When we are wronged or offended, we may claim and receive repayment through Jesus Christ. Also, He stands for the trespasser to fulfill everyone's claim against him. When we forgive others, God through Christ will restore our loss."

Sometimes we don't know what to pray to the Father about regarding a specific trespass. Jesus Christ is right at the throne, mediating and praying for us.

The trespass offering is also called a quilt offering (Leviticus 5:14–19). The Lord makes His life a quilt offering (Isaiah 53:10 NASB). This was concerned mainly with restitution. If you have not called on Christ, you will feel guilt. You know you should ask and you know you need Jesus.

God loves the sinner who hates sin as He does. He tells us He will forgive us our sins and cleanse us from all unrighteousness (1 John 1:9 The Message).

Be aware of those trespasses you commit against God, His holy things, and your fellow man. Make the effort to correct these, and then go to Jesus. We inevitably do wrong when we maintain relationships with other people. Make it right by apologizing and/or seeking forgiveness.

The sin offering actually refers to the confession of all we think, say, or do, not to mention the secret faults that displease God. Jesus is our sin offering to God. Our acts of repentance and confessing our sins enable us to offer our sins to God and seek His forgiveness.

We should seek cleansing from God. Whoever is not cleansed cannot have communion with God. You can't be committed to God like you should in this case.

The trespass offering represents the necessity of making restitution to the victim of your sins. Jesus made restitution for us so that we could be forgiven upon repentance. Likewise, we should make restitution when we sin against our fellow man. We should repent and confess. Then we should show love to our fellow man.

Don't allow any guilt over past or present sins to overcome you or weigh you down. Simply ask God and those you offend to forgive you. Keep God's promises in mind. He will meet your needs at the right time in the right way. He will guide and comfort you. Then joy and peace will return to you.

"I beseech you therefore, brethren, by the mercies of God, that you present your bodies a living sacrifice, holy, acceptable to God, which is your reasonable service" (Romans 12:1 NKJV).

CHAPTER THREE

Give Yourself Totally to God

Be a Complete Sacrifice

Since particular believers have confessed their sins against God and/or their fellow man, obtained forgiveness, and now received salvation, they are free to voluntarily and completely give their lives to God. The sacrifices were designed to transform the natural carnal person into an actual child of God.

The third offering that the people of Israel offered was a voluntary burnt offering of the whole body. It was the most complete of all the sacrifices because it was completely burned up. Only the skin was saved and given to the presiding priest. The purpose of this offering was to give everything to God. It is a freewill act of worship. It's a way of saying that you commit yourself to God. You had surrendered all the way. You are going to put all your faith in God. You are going to obey God all the way. This offering lets the offeror atone for the sin and thus gain acceptance from God.

Burnt offerings were the very first and most common type of offering made even before Leviticus. Noah and Abraham showed the Israelites the two meanings of the burnt offering. After the flood, Noah sacrificed numerous burnt offerings to God. As a result, God made a covenant promise to Noah and humankind to never again destroy every living thing by a flood. The people of Israel saw that a burnt offering was the way to avoid God's wrath and to obtain His favor. The blessing came because of the burnt offering and not humanity's good deeds. Abraham provided another view about what the burnt offering could do. God commanded him to offer Isaac, his only son, as a burnt offering on a mountain (Genesis 22). Abraham brought branches, a knife, and his son to the site. He knew God could raise Isaac from the dead. God stopped Abraham from slaying his son and provided a ram in his place. Earlier, God made a covenant with Abraham (Genesis 12:1–3). The people of Israel saw that the sacrificial animal died in place of the man just as the ram died in the place of Isaac. They also realized that something must happen in a greater way in the future.

Even though ancient Israelites did know God was at work in an unknown and mysterious way, they presented their burnt offerings so that they could avoid God's wrath and receive blessings.

Offering Procedure

The animal must be healthy and without blemishes or defects. God won't accept our spiritual offering with these.

Offerors could present an offering from a herd (bullock) or a flock (sheep or goat) of three years or younger, or they could present a bird (turtledove/pigeon). Each represented different levels of holdings and financial success. God wanted everyone to have the chance to offer a sacrifice whether they were rich, middle-class, or poor. This perfect willing sacrifice enabled the believer to consecrate himself totally as a living sacrifice to God. Children of God today offer their total spiritual lives to God.

The animal sacrificed must be perfect and blemish-free to be accepted by God. God wants our best. The offerors would purify themselves and bring the animals. They would lay their hands on the heads of the animals. In this act, they transferred their sins to the animals. They were personally involved in slaying, skinning, and preparing the sacrifices too. Thus, the killing of the animals showed that the offerors were making gifts of themselves and devoting their entire lives to God. The innards and legs were washed with water, after which the priest would arrange and burn all the pieces upon the altar. The priest performed the rituals and would place the blood on the altar.

The burnt offering reminded the offerors of their general state of sinfulness, not repentance for specific sins. The burnt offering "seems to provide the solution for man's fallen condition."

Leviticus 1:3, 5–9 tells us how the burnt offering was uniquely divided into five parts and burned totally. This is the only offering where the animal is completely burned up. However, the priest would get the skin.

The body of the animal was cut up into five parts consisting of the head, legs, innards, fat, and the remaining body. This dividing of the body parts makes the burnt offering very unique. The skin of the animal is the only part that is not consumed. The residing priest received that part as a fee for burning the five pieces as the sacrifice and offering blood on the altar. Each part is a similitude for various aspects of a person's life. Taken together, these reveal a quality of life totally dedicated to God.

There were other offerings given along with the burnt offering. The meal offering and peace offerings were included. Even a drink offering was made. Also, a burnt offering could be made in conjunction with the trespass offering, the sin offering, the freewill offering, and the new grain offering. This combination shows love for God and love for humankind.

Since you know God is true and holy, allow yourself to be fully consumed daily. He used a burnt offering to show Israel how great He really was for them. The prophets of Baal first called out to their god to burn its bull. Of course, it didn't answer. Elijah the prophet then had their burnt offering heavily drenched in water as it lay on the wood. Twelve stones were placed around the offering. This was done three times. He prayed to God. God completely burned the bull, the wood, and the stones. It even licked up all the water in the trench. When the people saw this, they cried out, "The LORD—he is God! The LORD—he is God!" God can do anything He pleases. As you give all your life to Him, He can use you to open the eyes and conviction of unbelievers, doubters, and lost sheep. You can remind others that God gives us His very best and expects that we totally devote our lives to Him (1 Kings 18:20–39 NLT). When you ask, God is ready to do your impossible. He is the one to be glorified and honored.

Therefore, offer yourself to God as those who have been brought from death to life, and offer the parts of your body to Him as instruments of righteousness. You are under grace (Romans 6:13; 8:5). Yield your hands, body, feet, voice, compassions, and desires to the Father so He will accomplish His final goals for our lives.

Prayer has taken the place of sacrifices. When everyone in Nineveh repented and fasted, God relented and did not bring the destruction He had threatened them with (Jonah 3:8–10).

"So here's what I want you to do, God helping you: Take your everyday ordinary life—your sleeping, eating, going-to-work, and walking-around life—and place it before God as an offering. Embracing what God does for us is the best thing you can do for Him" (Romans 12:1 The Message).

PART ONE – THE HEAD

Mental Activity, Decisions, and Thoughts

The head signifies one's thoughts and judgements. Every thought must be brought into control and obedience to Jesus Christ. Our mind is the battlefield where we decide what we think about. You want your thoughts to be in line with God's Word. Where the mind goes, the body follows. We become what we think (Proverbs 23:7). We decide what we are going to do and then go do it. Satan is trying very hard to put wrong thoughts into your mind through deception, lies, and misdirection. Because of human nature we don't want to give ourselves to God. We are filled with pride, self-will, and self-reliance. We make the mistake of not wanting God involved in everything. We tend to think we can handle things on our own. It is very important that you renew your mind when it comes to your finances, your health, your family, time management, vacations and recreations, your job, your future, and so much more. Bring your thoughts in line with the higher thoughts of God.

1. Obey the Living God

"Does the LORD delight in burnt offerings and sacrifices as much as in obeying the voice of the LORD? To obey is better than sacrifice; and to heed is better than fat rams" (1 Samuel 15:22).

"Whoever has my commands and obeys them, he is the one who loves me. If anyone loves me, he will obey my teaching. My Father will love him, and will come to him and make our home with him" (John 14:15, 21, 23).

"Go ahead, add your burnt offerings to your other sacrifices and eat the meat yourselves! For when I brought your ancestors out of Egypt and spoke to them, I did not just give them commands about burnt offerings and sacrifices, but I gave them this command: Obey me, and I will be your God and you will be my people. Walk in obedience to all I command you, that it will go well with you" (Jeremiah 7:21–23).

What is obedience?

It is a matter of listening to God and doing what He tells you to do even when you don't understand why, how, or when. Abraham set an eye-opening example for us. Abraham obeyed immediately and persistently.

He obeyed when he did not know where he was going. God made a very specific promise to Abraham. He believed everything God told him. He also obeyed when he did not know how God's will would be accomplished. Our faith is based on the faithfulness of God. He can do what He says. Faith asks, "How shall this be?" Abraham obeyed God by faith when he did not know why. God was working. Follow God even though you don't know why He is directing you. He will show you what He wants of you. God may ask you to leave your current family and friend circle. You may have to change jobs or cities. You may be guided to a different location. The Holy Spirit lets you know why to go, where to go, and when to go. You know God will work it out. Abraham obeyed God even though he did not know when God would fulfill His promises (Hebrews 11:8–19).

There are three lessons we can learn from Abraham. First, don't limit God (Psalm 78:41 NKJV). There is nothing God can't do. There are some things God will not do for you. God can change our minds so we know what He is really like. Just be available. Second, don't go beyond what God has asked. Stick with His Word. Don't put your faith in something that's not God's will. Also, if God has not promised it, let it go. If God doesn't promise it, you can't have faith in it. We should glorify God. We have to understand what God wants us to actually do and where to stop. About a year ago, I fully retired from teaching elementary special education. I had plenty of materials and supplies in storage. A new third-grade math-science teacher could use those supplies. So I told her I would give her the materials I had. I knew this was God's will for me. So I gave her all the math materials and science supplies I had. In talking to her, she revealed that the former teacher had cleared out everything in the classroom. She started preparing to set up her room in January after the Christmas break. So I figured that I could help her set the room up. That would be fun. However, she never asked me. I even volunteered. She sent a phone picture of the classroom she and her friend set up. They did a super job. They used a lot of the posters. Then I realized God only wanted me to provide her with my math supplies and materials. Third, we can learn to not worry about success. If it is God's will, everything will work out. We are called to be faithful to God. So we have to be patient with God when we don't always know the where, when, and how. This is true obedience.

Are you putting your job, family, position, money, or friendships before God? Do you hate others or wish others harm? Do you have romantic relations with people who aren't your mate? Do you participate in sex before marriage? Do you steal from others? Do you lie to others or misrepresent others? Do you desire the money, fame, car, house, job, and influence others have? Do you seek revenge when wronged? Do you not forgive others who lie or try to take all the credit for your work? This is not obeying God or loving your fellow man!

God is who we should worship.

God is the Holy Trinity consisting of God the Father, Jesus Christ, and the Holy Spirit. They are omnipotent (limitless power), omniscient (limitless knowledge), omnipresent (universal presence), immutable (incapable of change), and eternal (limitless life). There is one God who is of three eternal persons. God is three in one. They are the same in substance or essence, but they have distinct views and ways to participate in the love quest for us. Genesis makes three references to God with the pronoun *us*. "Let us make man" (Genesis 1:26). "Man has become like us" (Genesis 3:22). "Come, let us go down and there confuse their language" (Genesis 11:17). Their teamwork is perfect and inspiring. Their combined supporting love and power will get you through anything. The Father, Jesus the Son, and the Holy Spirit are coequal in love, holiness, purpose, devotion, concern, and power. Each shows these in different ways. They relate to one another in true love and perfect harmony. Trust is the foundation of their relationship.

Let's take a closer look at four main areas of God the Father's focus in the trinity. First, God the Father has the fantastic overview of everything with final authority. Jesus prayed to Him very often for answers and help. We also pray to the Father by using the model prayer (Matthew 6:6–14). Ask the Father for what you need, even though He already knows what you need. He is the one to give final glory to since He oversees everything and everyone. Everything comes from Him, and everything goes back to Him in the end. Jesus's final move is to glorify the Father by putting all things back into the Father's hands. God created the world for His glory. He wants us to truly know Him and love Him. We are meant to show others who God is really like. The Father is the final person we are to glorify. He is the one most worthy of praise. Jesus tells us to glorify the Father in everything.

Jesus was sent to earth as a newborn baby by Father God. He sends the Holy Spirit to those who accept Christ's sacrifice. He gave an unlimited amount of the Spirit to Jesus at His baptism. He told the world that He was very pleased with His Son, Jesus. Father God forgives us when we repent. Jesus presented Himself to the Father after His resurrection so that He would be glorified as He was before the foundation of the world. He chooses those He wants to include within His family. Jesus desires and works to keep those called by Father God to receive eternal life. A close relation with the Father is most important. We are reconciled to the Father by the blood of Jesus. Since the Father hates evil, you need to break the wall down that separates you from the holy Father (Romans 5:10). We need to be reconciled to Him.

Jesus prayed to Father God while on earth so many times a day. Only the Father knows the day and hour when the end of the age will come. He is preparing the holy city, Jerusalem, for the saints that are found in the Lamb's book of life and that possess the Holy Spirit. It is so rewarding to realize that God has the power, love, and desire to accomplish everything that is needed. He knows all, sees all, and is everywhere.[2]

Second, the Father initiates relationships and action. He is the one who calls us to be part of His family as adopted children. He sends the Holy Spirit to give us help and instruction about spiritual matters. This seals us as family. He adds to the church through the Holy Spirit. Jesus seeks to keep those who are called. God loved us first. God the Father started the relationship with us. He loves us and wants us to live fulfilling and meaningful lives. The Father and Jesus sent the Comforter, the Holy Spirit. He wants to know you, and He wants to bring you into His family for eternal life in the kingdom of heaven.

---

[2] Pastor Bill Bradford, "The Father Has Authority Over Everything," Worldwide Church of God, Shreveport, LA, May 1983.

He is active and interested in variety. He has a sense of humor, and He likes exciting people. He is the one who assigns responsibilities and purpose in our lives.

He has chosen you to fulfill certain jobs now and in the world tomorrow. It is the Father's and Jesus's will that you have eternal life. We will have responsibilities in the New Jerusalem. The earth will be purified. Then the center of the universe is moved or extended to earth because Father God and Jesus Christ come here.

He loves order. He gives direction to the family so that we keep doing our very best. He will accept those who look like Jesus's righteousness and reflect Jesus's love and character.

He loves to expose us to a variety of cultural experiences though great music, art, literature, and sports. He loves a variety of people with different backgrounds and cultures. That's why He created variety. He enjoys music and singing that honors and glorifies Him.[3]

Third, God the Father develops and executes plans with eternal outcomes and effects. He makes and implements future planning that involves us now. The Father masterminded the whole sequence of creation. The angels, the twenty-four elders, and the four living creatures were created first. Then God gave the actual creation of the coming universe to Jesus. Lastly, the spiritual creation of humankind was devised. Father God and the Son together made the plans, diagram, and format for the universe. Jesus Christ used this blueprint in creating the universe.

This was outstanding teamwork. Jesus has tremendous, unbelievable, and unmeasurable mental powers. All Jesus had to do was speak it, and it was done. Jesus just spoke it into existence. Even today Jesus heals us by His Word in heaven. Then Jesus finished earth in six days by separating land from water and creating plants, animals, and humankind.

---

[3] Pastor Bill Bradford, "The Father Initiates Relationships and Action," Worldwide Church of God, Shreveport, LA, May 1983.

The Father sent Jesus to earth with the message of the gospel. He originated the message. The Father wants everyone to believe in Jesus (John 6:29). He set in motion the plan of salvation through Christ. Jesus volunteered to die for humankind. God's will is that none be lost and that all be raised up. Father God is using the new covenant to bring us into the family of God. The Father formulated the message Christ gave us about the kingdom of God. Jesus gave humanity the understanding and special wisdom and knowledge of God. This included the way of life to free us from the penalty of death and make us successful.

Father God assigns responsibilities in the kingdom of God (Mark 10:35–40). Our individual assignments will be given by the Father. Jesus makes sure we are properly trained for it. He is building the holy city in the New Jerusalem (Revelation 21:2, 10–27). There are many mansions in the Father's house. The training we receive from Jesus and the Holy Spirit prepares us to fulfill our responsibilities (John 14:2–3 NLT). God the Father chose us, adopted us, and then gave us grace.

Our Father God has developed an ever-growing, challenging, and exciting training program for His family for all eternity. God is guiding and leading us to universal goals forever.

Some will hold key positions in His government during the one-thousand-year reign of King Jesus Christ on earth. This will be great training for us. Then a new heaven and a new earth will come since the first earth will have passed away. He will dwell on earth with His family. He will be our God, and we will be His people (Revelation 21:3 NKJV). He looks forward to this moment. You are royalty and destined to rule with our Savior. You should be so thankful that God has such great plans for you. You will always be growing, learning, and developing new responsibilities. You will glorify God and enjoy Him forever.[4]

Fourth, God the Father honors and glorifies Jesus Christ. He told the world "This is my Son, whom I love; with you I am well pleased" (Luke

---

[4] Pastor Bill Bradford, "The Father Develops and Executes Plans with Eternal Outcomes and Effects," Worldwide Church of God, Shreveport, LA, May 1983.

3:21–22 NKJV). He glorifies Jesus (John 8:54–56; Acts 3:13). The Father reveals there is no other name under heaven by which you can be saved but Christ. Because Jesus died for us, everything is possible. Our Father gave Jesus Christ judgment over the living, the church, and the wicked. The Father validates Jesus's testimony (John 8:16–18). He also testified about Jesus being sent from heaven (John 5:36–37a). Jesus does what He sees the Father do. All things have been laid in Jesus's hands and committed to Jesus by the Father (Matthew 11:27; John 3:35 NKJV). Healing comes by Jesus's name and faith in Him (Acts 3:16).[5]

Father God lovingly resurrected Jesus to confirm He is the Messiah and the Son of God (Romans 8:11, 13). Eternal life is made available for all humankind. Once we confess our sins and accept Jesus' sacrifice as payment for our debt, we become adopted children in the God family. The love, grace, and mercy of God lead us to fulfill our purpose to serve and glorify God.

God the Father placed Jesus as the center of the plan of salvation before the world was formed. God's wrath is on anyone who does not believe in the Son (John 3:36). Our Father shows who is greatest among His servants, the prophets Moses and Elijah. Of course, it is Jesus the Son (Matthew 17:1–8). Through Jesus's name, we receive forgiveness of sins and grace. Jesus is honored by the Father because He entrusted all judgment on Him (John 5:22–23 The Message). The Father will make sure all bow before Christ since He created the universe. He is King of Kings and Lord of Lords. Our Father has complete and total confidence in Jesus Christ. Jesus is coequal with God the Father. Jesus is God.

The Holy Spirit also brings honor and glory to Jesus Christ. That's His main purpose. He highlights the work of Jesus. This means He teaches, reminds, and informs us about Jesus. He guides us into all truth. He points out what Jesus said that became doctrine. He reviews history and prophetic things to come concerning Jesus. The Holy Spirit draws us to Jesus based on who the Father calls. Jesus then works with us to confirm and assure

---

[5] Pastor Bill Bradford, "The Father Honors and Glorifies Jesus Christ," Worldwide Church of God, Shreveport, LA, May 1983.

our success. The Holy Spirit reproduces the character of Jesus in us. The fruits of the Spirit become parts of our character. He is also our advocate, helper, counselor, and comforter. The Spirit endows us with gifts to enable us to serve others and God (John 14:16–26 NASB).

The three of them share incredible teamwork. They possess an indescribable level of complete trust, confidence, reliance, and awareness. They act as one, and each knows what the others desire, need, and think because of the love among them. They express cooperation and unity so naturally. "We have been chosen and loved by the Father, redeemed and blessed by the Son, and empowered by the Holy Spirit. Filled with wonder that we are so important that each person in the Godhead actively participated in winning us salvation … We are God's dearly loved children." They have been doing this all along. Their loving relationship ensures they only do what's best for each one of us. God truly loves us. All three are equally holy, righteous, and loving.

When Jesus shed His blood for you, you were redeemed. He provided forgiveness for your sins, and he placed grace on you. His will became known to you. Jesus bought the church, justified us, freed us from our sins, and made peace for us as a beginning gesture.

The Holy Spirit opens our minds so that we understand the truth of the gospel and opens our hearts so that we believe in the gospel. He helps us to understand. When the Holy Spirit finishes His work, we can believe and call on the name of the Lord for salvation. Otherwise, a person would never come to faith in Christ. We are born again by the Spirit of God. We are taught the things of the Spirit, and we are reminded about what Jesus said. He speaks words from the Father. He lives in you. He seals us. The Holy Spirit is the spiritual power source. He releases His power into our lives to help us serve and live godly lives. He guides us rightly since He knows the Lord's will for us. The Spirit's presence in us shows us that we belong to God. Salvation is guaranteed. He also intercedes in prayer for us.

Later I will discuss the ways Jesus the Son is at the center of our lives. I will discuss why He is the center of our lives. In addition, I will focus on some of the things He did in the past, does now, and will do in the future. It's impossible to show them all. (See appendix 1, "Jesus Is Our Center of Life.") You will learn about the glorious things He does.

The Holy Spirit is our secret weapon. Let Him lead and guide you (Psalm 31:3) to do God's will. The Holy Spirit knows the Father's will.

As we come to learn more about how great and loving God is, we realize that we have only a glimpse of what and who God really is. There is so much to who and what God is. Learning about God is an ongoing process. The more you learn about God, the more you realize there is so much more to learn. But when we see the Father and Jesus in their glorified state, we can make a great jump to understand more. As we see God work on His plan of salvation for humankind, we will never stop praising God for all eternity. The angels, the twenty-four elders, and the four living creatures have been doing this since they were created billions of years ago.

God is so much that He is able to help us with anything. Of course, no matter what our situations are, God is able and willing to help. He has many names that describe His character. He has unlimited power. Time and space have no bearing on Him.

A. We should obey God rather than people.

We owe our very lives to God. You have an obligation to obey God's instructions and directions.

After he was humbled, King Nebuchadnezzar of the Babylon Empire named God as the Most High, who is sovereign over the kingdoms of mortals. God gives kingdoms to anyone He wishes and sets over them the lowliest of people. He has an eternal dominion that endures from generation to generation. The king pointed out that the Most High does as He pleases with the powers of heaven and the peoples of earth. He praised God as the King of heaven because everything He does is right and all His ways are just (Daniel 4:2–3, 17, 34–37).

God describes Himself as "The LORD, the LORD God, compassionate, and gracious God, slow to anger, abounding in love and faithfulness, maintaining love to thousands, and forgiving wickedness, rebellion and sin. Yet He does not leave the guilty unpunished" (Exodus 34:5–7 NLT).

God demands obedience because He deserves it. He is such a powerful, loving, and merciful being. He is the one who starts the relationship because of His deep love for you. Obeying God is the first step to having a relationship with Him. It is an outward expression of your love for God. Real love will lead us to do what God wants you to do without questioning the greatness and ability of God Himself. This is an outward expression of the real thing (2 John 5–6). Remember that God is always right and just. He wants the best for you, and He knows what's best for you.

As adults, we do what our employers tell us to do. First, we do so because we have to if we want to keep our jobs. Then we obey because we need to get paychecks to pay our bills. Third, we follow instructions because we want to be outstanding and loyal employees. Christians obey God to keep a great relationship with Him.

Why did you obey your parents? We learn obedience as children. You feel you have to obey them or fear what will happen if you don't. You don't want a spanking after all. You also seek praise or rewards. You want a favorite toy or gift. You also obeyed your parents because you wanted to please them. You have love and respect for your parents too. Christians obey God because He loved us first (John 3:16). Thus, we love God back. Thus, we obey God. We come to realize that God wants the very best for us.[6]

B. Obeying God Is So Important

Obeying God is the most important act of faith and trust you can make. It is the foundation and cornerstone of your relationship with the Father and Jesus Christ. "Obedience is the only thing God has ever required of man."

---

[6] John Moore, "Obedience," Preacher Faith Community, Shreveport, LA, October 28, 2016.

For without obedience to God, there is no real relationship. You come up short. If one of them tells you to do something and you don't carry out that command, you are separating yourself. Remember you benefit from obeying. God can tell you what needs to be done in many ways. He mostly uses His Word. He can use others to say or do something to influence. He also uses circumstances and situations to get your attention.

Real love will lead us to do as He tells us through listening, helping, serving, encouraging, and giving our time, money, and abilities.

He created a sacrificial system to remind Israel they needed to get right with Him, the almighty Lord. He rejected and abandoned that generation because of disobedience. He held on to a remnant.

Joshua told the eastern tribes returning home from the long war to "be very careful to keep the commandment and law that Moses the servant of the LORD gave you: to love the LORD your God, to walk in all His ways, to obey his commands, to hold fast to him and to serve him with all your heart and all your soul." Then Joshua blessed those three tribes (Joshua 22:5). If you want to live a long and prosperous life, do what God tells you to do. Also, do it quickly. Delayed obedience is disobedience.

Without God in your life, it is meaningless. A lifestyle of obedience is a major key to answered prayer. Obey and pray. Pray and obey. "You must have the confidence to obey God and leave the consequences to Him." You also must have the desire to put Him first in your time, effort, energy, and talents.

Jesus Christ learned obedience by suffering. He was obedient and did as the Father instructed Him. The Father sent Him to accomplish several things. His perfect obedience makes us acceptable and justified to the Father.

To obey God is a mental decision you make. It is a decision to go beyond emotions. "We must own our emotions and not allow them to own us." People may want to forgive friends for hurting them. These people must come to see that good intentions are not obedience. "If you just listen but don't obey, it really doesn't help us or glorify God." It will take mental toughness to not procrastinate and make excuses.

You know God wants, requires, and deserves obedience from you. Every time you obey, you offer up a spiritual sacrifice to God.

So you are actually obeying three persons. First, you obey the Father God as He calls you, appoints your purposes, and gives eternal life. You also obey Jesus since He set the example of a sinless life on earth to become a perfect sacrifice. Finally, you obey the Holy Spirit as He instructs you, inspires you, guides you, and empowers you to do the Father's will.

The real question is this: "Why not obey God?"

C. God learns a lot about you as He sees you follow His instructions.

God is constantly evaluating your reactions to instructions, situations, and changing trials and temptations. "God's only pain is to be doubted; God's only pleasure is to be believed." All God wants to know is that you completely trust Him to do what's right and just for you. He realizes the following about you:

- He is impressed that you follow Jesus's example of obedience to Him.
- You are surrendering your will to Him more and more.
- You understand you are required to act in faith and steadily move in greater obedience.
- He sees you obey more as you know Him more. Thus, you love Him more.
- You actually trust and lean on Him to do what's right and just.
- You take the time to read and study the scriptures for understanding and instruction.
- You really revere and respect Him.
- You realize the Spirit of God gives you the desire and ability to obey Him.

- You know nothing is impossible for Him. God still performs miracles.
- You know everything will work out as you listen and obey.

Of course, we must ask God to give us the vision and desire to keep doing these things. We need God's involvement in our lives to accomplish each of these. Ask God for guidance to keep doing these things.

D. Rewards of Obedience

First of all, you desire to obey God just because of who He truly is to you. Then you see you receive blessings for your devotion. Some of those blessings and rewards are listed here. "You will be making major and minor adjustments. You are moving from your way of thinking to God's way of thinking. You are moving from your purposes to working on God's purposes. You are moving from doing things your way to doing things God's way. You are moving from human values to God's values."[7] As you make adjustments, you'll realize the reward of experiencing God is worth the changes. Here are just a few of the blessings you will receive because you do what God tells you.

- You will live a long prosperous life since you are doing what is good and right in the eyes of God (Deuteronomy 12:28 The Message).
- You are blessed and become a blessing to others. Things will go well with you and your children.
- Eternal life is the final reward when you know Jesus Christ (John 17:2–3 NASB).
- You have a growing relationship with God.
- You won't fail. God is for you. God is with you. God is in you (Isaiah 41:10 NASB).
- You receive the Holy Spirit because you repented and asked for forgiveness.
- You bear much fruit as you follow God's lead and directions.

---

[7] Henry and Richard Blackaby and Claude King, *Experiencing God* (Nashville: LifeWay Press, 2007), 161.

- Jesus Christ and the Father will come to live in you by the Holy Spirit (John 14:15, 21, 23).
- You are abiding in Christ and are in fellowship with God.
- You belong to His family, and you are now part of the church family. You are a citizen of heaven.
- You are a friend and coheir with Jesus.
- You have great peace, joy, happiness, and hope.
- Your prayers are answered.
- Wealth and success come from your obedience.
- Obedience is a seed you have sown. Great things keep coming your way.
- The Holy Spirit continues to give you the desire and ability to walk in obedience to God's will. He even reveals what is the Father's will and purpose concerning you.
- You have a more intimate relationship with God. You are truly abiding in Jesus, and you have fellowship with God constantly. This is what He really wants.
- You have great confidence in God. He always does what He says He's going to do. You know that everything God wants for you will work out. You know God does what's right and just every time.
- You have victory over sin and everything the devil throws at you. You have victory in your spiritual warfare.
- God reveals Himself more and more to you.

E. Not obeying God will cost you dearly.

"Disobedience is always more costly than obedience." Here are some of the reasons you will have an unsatisfying and unfruitful life.

- He simply requires your obedience. Many things you do will not turn out for the best. The money, wealth, power, and influence you have will still make your life less meaningful. You have a very negative relationship with God.

- You know God exist, but you won't admit it to yourself. You still want to have a relationship with the supreme being. You deny the fact that you are wired to worship God.
- You miss the hundreds of blessings God has to offer.
- You tell God that you can make it on your own and you don't need Jesus.
- Since you have rejected God, you walk down the broad wrong way. You do not have a love for the truth.
- You are putting your trust in yourself, others, and/or things instead of God.
- You can't live a moral life on your own. You need Jesus's help, but you won't ask for it.
- You are bringing judgment down on yourself, and you will perish eternally in hell.
- Since you are putting someone or something in front of God, you continue to suffer penalties and hurt. You'd rather sacrifice your future for the immediate satisfaction of prejudice, adultery, alcohol, drugs, hatred, unforgiveness, wealth, pride, power, etc.
- Submitting to your carnal lusts and worldly pleasures will only end in eternal death.
- You are at the mercy of Satan, who wants to destroy you. You are destroying your chances for everlasting life with God.
- You lack understanding and judgment about what's really important in life—eternal life with the Father, Jesus Christ, the Holy Spirit, and fellow saints.
- You do not know God and do not obey the gospel of Jesus Christ. Thus, you will pay the penalty of eternal destruction, away from the presence of the Lord and from the glory of His power (2 Thessalonians 1:8, 9).

The consequences of disobedience are very severe and everlasting. However, there is always hope. Turn to God if you never have before, or return to God if you once knew Him. Repent and confess your sins to God. Accept Jesus' death on the cross as payment of your sins. Turn your life around with the most important decision you can ever make. God changes your life when you set aside your own agendas, take Him at His Word, and obey Him. You can get help from Jesus and Holy Spirit. Have respect and reverence. Ask what God wants of you. "The whole duty of man is to fear God and keep His commands" (Ecclesiastics 12:13).

2. Know Jesus and His Ways

"But grow in the grace and knowledge of our Lord and Savior Jesus Christ. To him be glory both now and forever" (2 Peter 3:18)

"I want you to show love, not offer sacrifices. I want you to know me more than burnt offerings" (Hosea 6:6 NLT).

Your goal is to move beyond knowing about God to actually knowing God personally. Before you can truly worship God, you must know God and His ways. Before you can know God, you must study the Word, have real experiences, and allow God to reveal Himself to you. Reading and studying the Word is the most direct way to understand our Lord and Savior, Jesus Christ. You can also listen to and see sermons by way of CDs, videos, radio shows, cell phones, and television programs. The Gospels reveal a lot of firsthand information about Jesus. You can also get to know God by being around others who know Him well and live like Christ in the way they relate to others.

Decide what works best for your learning. We learn by reading, listening, discussing, and doing. What combination of these styles best fits you? Use these to know God better.

Having a closer relationship with God is fueled by what you know, understand, believe, and do about your awareness of God. This is rewarding because you are deepening your relationship with Jesus. You are trusting Jesus more and more to be there for you in any difficult and challenging situation.

Your experiences with Jesus help you come to great conclusions, decide to take God at His Word, trust God to keep all His promises, remember that He will never leave you, and recognize the fact that His love for you is deep, forever, and unconditional.

Over the years of direct experiences, situations, and answered prayer, you have come to know Jesus. Go back in your life. Recall the many times of miraculous help and healings, heart-rendering situations you went through, and temptations you had to fight, not to mention the anger, depression, anxiety, health problems, financial problems, and selfishness you had to battle. Jesus brought you through all these situations. Plus He is helping you now. Since He is helping you in these things, He wants you to trust Him completely. Since you know Him, you can believe Him. You should view Jesus with more awe and dedication. You will relate with Him at a high degree of devotion and worship. Here are some truths you should know concerning Jesus Christ.

Jesus is the Christ, the Son of God. Jesus is God. Peter pointed out that "we have come to believe and know that you are the Holy One of God" (John 6:68–69). Jesus told the Jews that He is from God (John 7:28–29 NASB). The Holy Spirit opens our minds to really see that Jesus is the Son of God. The Gospels testify to this. Because of His death and resurrection, salvation has come to everyone. Humankind has been redeemed. After Jesus was baptized, the Father said, "You are my Son, whom I love, with you I am well pleased" (Luke 3:22). His resurrection opened the door for eternal life and the way to serving others. So you know that Jesus is God.

Jesus is love. In spite of the sin we daily commit as human beings, He forgives us. He continues to love us. Everything He does for us is out of deep love. Nothing and no one can separate us from the love of Jesus. He is the reason for our relationship with the Father. God's nature is love—giving, serving, and helping. So if you love others, you know Jesus. The nature of humility is also there. Jesus even prays for us when we don't know what to say. He died for us, lives for us now, and includes us in ruling the world of the future. He is full of compassion and mercy (1 Corinthians 13:4–8 NKJV). True love does not act unbecomingly; it does not seek its own. It is not provoked, and it does not take into account a wrong suffered. Knowing we are loved and accepted no matter what is a relief. We only understand a little of how much Jesus actually loves us. He knows we are works in progress. Everything God does for us is for our good. Consider Lionel Richie's song "Jesus is Love."

Jesus is in us and is living that way of love. Jesus is with us. Jesus is for us. Jesus is in us. Jesus will go about loving and helping others when you yield to Him. His righteousness will be seen in you. Live by the faith and love of Jesus. God's character is the way of love. He has much concern for us. So as Jesus lives in you, His nature of concern about others will come out more and more. With God's Spirit, you will enjoy actual fellowship with the Father and Son, Jesus Christ. We have fellowship with fellow Christians through Christ. Live by the faith of Jesus so He can live His life through you. We are then walking with Christ. That means we are walking in the light and love.

Jesus never leaves you. He helps you in all your time of trouble, trials, and temptations. At times, He carries you through moments of weakness. There is nothing we can't face when we know the one in whom we believe. God then uses that experience to help others who are going through the same thing. No matter what is happening to you, Jesus is right there alongside of you always. He is faithful to you. He is completely trustworthy. He will not let you down. Jesus has your back. He loves us. This is the main promise we lean on.

Jesus uses His authority to heal the body, the mind, and the soul. He wants you to be healthy, whole, and balanced. This involves our physical, spiritual, mental, emotional, friendship, and financial needs. All you have to do is call on His name. Throughout the Gospels, Jesus healed people with many disabilities and sicknesses and even brought people back from death. He drove out wicked spirits. His mission was to proclaim the good news to the poor. He still wants to free those whose ways and thoughts keep them entangled and locked in hate, anger, pain, fear, and low self-esteem. He wants to keep you from drinking the poison of bitterness, resentment, and unforgiveness. Jesus seeks to open our eyes to more spiritual truth. He works to set us free (Luke 4:18–19 NLT).

Jesus keeps all His promises made to you. He has not failed you yet and never will. He promises to always love you unconditionally. He is always faithful to you as He promised. He provides for us in His way and in His time. He promised He would never leave us. God promised to complete the work He started in you (Philippians 1:6). These are only a few of the many promises so that you can abide in Him. He forgives us of sin. Jesus is a shield to you since you take refuge in Him. He gives us our daily bread since we focus on His kingdom. God has made more than a thousand to you. He keeps every one of them. Trust in His faithfulness to His Word.

Jesus prepares you to minister to others using your talents and abilities. The Holy Spirit gives those spiritual gifts and motivates us to accomplish on behalf of the work of God. You have been gifted with several talents, abilities, understanding, wisdom, and time. Ask God to help you do your best with these. Be willing to use them to help others. We are called to do something. Ask God for a passion to serve. Seek to serve the needs of others as He did. Ask Him to show you where and how you can serve those in your church and the greater community. Be a doer. That's how you grow. Jesus is getting you ready to serve more and more. The Holy Spirit gives you the talents and gifts to fulfill your purpose in serving.

Jesus wants all those whom the Father calls to succeed and accept eternal life. We are under His care and guidance (John 17:3). Jesus is in the middle of the effort of getting things done in your life. The Father sees our needs and has the plan. Jesus provides the skills and know-how. The Holy Spirit inspires you with desire, zeal, and energy so that you can get your work done. You will succeed in the purpose revealed to you. So the Father draws us to Christ by the Holy Spirit.

Jesus guides you to Himself—the real light, the real vine, the real bread from heaven, and the real source of eternal life. He and the Holy Spirit work in unison to keep you walking the right path.

Jesus will return to earth as the King of Kings and Lord of Lords. So too, He will be the judge of mankind in the last days with justice. He will also provide our future rewards. He plans for us to rule beside Him tomorrow and forever.

Jesus charges you to do your part and preach the gospel to the world. He uses your ministry of service as you share your experiences with unbelievers and those who don't know about Him. Share your journey, your weaknesses, and how God has gotten you where you are today. Tell others the good news about the wonderful grace of God. Tell your story.

Jesus knows what's best and right for you. You should be excited about knowing that God "knows exactly what is going to happen and is right there with us, helping us and directing us."

Jesus is the source of our peace, joy, confidence, and hope. You know Jesus is for us. Jesus is the head of the church. He assigns responsibilities to each member of the church family so that we can accomplish His will. He knows what's best for His church. His church will be presented without blemishes to Father God.

Jesus has overcome sin, death, the world, and Satan for us. His life, death, and resurrection ensured our victory. You will succeed. The war is won. So you can fight with confidence and assurance.

To know Christ is to perceive what He is saying to us through His words and the inspiration of the Holy Spirit. As you desire to know Jesus better and more deeply, you encounter several revelations.

First, you will learn about yourself as well as Jesus. You learn your sins. You will fall very short of the perfect loving Father. You need the Spirit and Jesus' help to keep the old self buried and to live anew according to the Holy Spirit (Romans 8:10).

Second, you recognize that Jesus' life was meant to prepare you for eternal life with Him. He wants you to share the gospel with others out of love. He wants you to prosper and be in health. We know that God gives us everything and that we need to do His will. He has specific purposes for you.

Third, we realize Jesus got along with people of varying backgrounds and cultures—the common man, the disabled, women, teaches, sinners, and children. He was approachable. Therefore, He wants you to get along with various people too. Don't look down on others, but seek to serve. Be approachable too.

Fourth, as you know Jesus, you find out His nature, His character, His values, His thoughts, and His ways. Your respect and love for Him deepens. He does so much for us. He is interested in everyone whom the Father calls and who believes in Him. The will of the Father is that you have eternal life. He knows how to guide us into true success. He looks forward to revealing more about Himself to you. This is serious Bible study.

Fifth, when considering the character of Jesus, you should be very excited. Each one of these should come to mind as you recall occasions, experiences, or situations where you know Jesus was in the middle of it. Jesus is love, joy, peace, patience, kindness, faith, goodness, gentility, and self-control. These are also the fruits of the Spirit. The Father, Jesus, and the Spirit are in a circular relationship of love, holiness, and righteousness. Our personal lives (and those of family and friends) should witness and testify that Jesus is all of these.

Sixth, His overall mission is to proclaim freedom for the prisoners, recover the sight of the spiritually blind, and release the oppressed (Luke 4:18–19).

Seven, Knowing Jesus better is an ongoing process. The more you know Him, the more you realize there is so much more to learn. We are to grab as many fragments of knowledge concerning Christ Jesus as humanly possible. You have only glimpsed the tip of an enormous iceberg regarding Jesus and God. Keep desiring to better understand Jesus each day. Ask that you progressively become more intimately acquainted with Jesus. The Spirit in us is our capacity to know God and to relate to God.

Eight, as you get to know Jesus better, you should not get puffed-up or bigheaded. You talk about God and not yourself. You will constantly talk about how great God is. You remind yourself that nothing is impossible to God. You remember God is busy doing good for those who love Him. He will finish what He started. You don't compare yourself with other human beings. You are accomplishing good things only because of God's gifts of grace and talents. You don't look down on others unless you are pulling them up.

Nine, knowing Jesus causes you to act and behave better. Your life totally changes. Faith without works is dead. If you don't act on what you understand, you only possess information. It can give you a big head. Faith without works is dead. Sometimes just knowing about Jesus can lead to vanity. Remember that whatever you get done, it's because of Jesus. Don't judge others. You are in close fellowship with God because you believe Him, you obey Him, you trust Him, and you respect Him. Your zeal for God is clearer. People should say you are the salt of the earth, a light in a dark world, and one who walks the way of God. All of this is done because of God's gifts of grace, forgiveness, and love. Let Jesus live through you. This glorifies Jesus, who glorifies the Father.

Ten, Knowing Jesus helps us realize that we are nothing without Him. His ways and thoughts are so much higher than ours. He actually gave His blood on our behalf. This onetime sacrifice paid our debt since He was both God and man. He lived a perfect and righteous life on earth for us. He never sinned. There is no comparison to Jesus. We are mere mortal human beings. We can die in so many ways. He freed us from the law. He loves us so much that He wants us to become more like Him—righteous, holy, and eternal. This is why we repent and confess our sins more easily. His love is very real and true. We need Jesus in the center of our lives.

Jesus expects you to follow His example of love. This means you must meet the needs of others. How do we show the world the love of God?

We do so by meeting the needs of the people around us. Are you meeting the needs of the people God brings into your life? Are you loving God by loving your neighbor? Ask God to show you how to meet the needs of your family, your coworkers, even your neighbors. Then go out there, and love your neighbor as yourself.

As you desire to know Jesus, you glorify God. We also glorify God when we live lives that are worthy of His calling and when you help people praise God. Lift up Jesus' name.

You recognize that God really is all-knowing and all-powerful and thus does what is right and just every time for you. Our purpose is to know God. There is nothing greater than knowing Jesus. When you list and focus on what you know, you realize you know Jesus better than you thought. You have daily experiences with Him. You are in a close relationship and communion with Jesus. Keep striving to know Him even better. Strive to abide in Christ. Just ask to be with Jesus more and more.

Thank God for where you are in knowing Jesus. You are a special person to Jesus. You are His adopted brother or sister. So He loves us even more deeply.

If you know God, you'll love Him. If you love God, you'll love your neighbor. You'll follow Jesus's example (1 John 2:3–6 The Message).

As you know Jesus, you will call upon Him more by using His many titles, positions of authority, and involvement with creation. In your prayers you can address Him as the anointed one, the only begotten Son, the Alpha and Omega, the Son of Man, the author and perfecter of our faith, King of Kings, Lord of Lords. Jesus is our Savior, King, and High Priest.

When you pray to God, you can address Jesus according to who He is and what He has done and is doing. Since God is three in one, we get to talk to our heavenly Father and almighty God. We realize the Holy Spirit is our helper and counselor. If you want a very thorough listing of names, titles, and descriptions of God, read *Experiencing God: Knowing and Doing the Will of God.*[8]

You know Jesus is the bread of life, the light to the world, the gate, the Good Shepherd, the resurrection and the life, the way and the truth and the light, and the true vine as mentioned in the book of John. Giving your life to knowing Christ intimately is worth it because of the wonders of His person. Seek to know Him more deeply. Seek a closer relationship with Jesus just because you love Him and want to find favor with Him (Exodus 33:13).

Ask the Holy Spirit to reveal more and more of Jesus to you. You'll want more firsthand experiences with Him. You will desire to keep going as you grow in God. This makes you want to be in His presence. This helps you to stay focused as you pray and read God's Word.

"What is more, I consider everything a loss because of the surpassing worth of knowing Christ Jesus my Lord, for whose sake I have lost all things ... I want to know Christ—yes, to know the power of His resurrection and participation in his suffering, somehow, attaining to the resurrection from the dead" (Philippians 3:8, 10).

When you take the time to know Jesus, you offer a spiritual sacrifice.

"And this is real and eternal life: That they know you, The one and only true God, and Jesus, whom you sent" (John 17:3 The Message).

---

[8] Henry Blackaby, Richard Blackaby, and Claude King, *Experiencing God* (Nashville: LifeWay Press, 2011), 268–69.

3. Keep a Repentant Mind and Heart

"The sacrifice you desire is a broken spirit. You will not reject a broken and repentant heart, O God" (Psalm 51:17 NLT).

"These are the ones I look on with favor; those who are humble and contrite in spirit, and who trembles at my word" (Isaiah 66:2b).

"Therefore, as God's chosen people, holy and dearly beloved, clothe yourself with compassion, kindness, humility, gentleness and patience" (Colossians 3:12).

God wants you to be humble before Him. He knows this mind-set is best if you want to keep your close relationship growing. He hears the prayers of the humble person.

Since you know Jesus, you have a repentant mind. You repent of your sins and confess daily. You ask for forgiveness as well because of Jesus's blood. You have a humble mind as well.

Repentance is the first step to salvation and eternal life. It is an ongoing process of confessing your sins to God. It must be sincere and real (Joel 2:12–13; 2 Chronicles 7:14).

Having a repentant mind is a mental decision you made. No matter how successful you are, God is helping you. You are fighting to keep the old self buried, the one who wants to be vain, and you strive to live as your new self through the Holy Spirit. During a Bible study, a preaching elder in Baltimore shared with me some interesting views about repentance.

First, you have an informed mind. Knowing about how great the love of God is and about the fact that you will fall short helps you stay humble. See your spiritual poverty. Realize that you need spiritual food and are unworthy of the grace given you. You keep returning to God. You understand what repentance means. You delight in God's commands. You work because of what you know about God, not merely because of your emotions. You know the battle over sin begins in your mind.

Second, you have a determined mind. You keep getting up when you fall. You keep walking down the straight and narrow path. You know God is there to pick you up and help you through all your problems. Even when you fall short in prayer and Bible study, you come back to God the next day. This constant seeking of God is your bread and butter. Your relationship with God is the most important thing. You always ask God to restore your love and dedication to Him. His purpose for you is mind-boggling.

Third, you have a joyful mind. You are full of the joy of God. You gladly receive the Word of God. Be excited in learning eternal knowledge from God. He removes burdens and anxieties from you and lightens your load. As you realize God forgives, joy and peace become parts of your life more and more.

Fourth, you have an obedient mind (John 15:10 NASB). As you learn and understand God's way, you work on applying His way in your everyday life. You bring forth the fruit of repentance. You do what God tells you to do faster and better. God requires you to follow His instructions and guidance.

Fifth, you have a growing mind. The previously outlined mind-sets are evident in your life. You can see change. You keep developing a closer personal relationship with God. You seek to deepen, broaden, and heighten that relationship (Ephesians 3:18–19). God reveals how to do this. You realize there is so much more to learn. You stay excited about knowing God better and better.

Six, you also have a renewed mind. You are changing and growing in your truth about Jesus. You see what Jesus did, and that has set you on the right path to pleasing God. You fight negative and harmful thoughts. You seek and cling to positive ways of thinking. You are trying to lay aside your wicked and selfish desires.[9]

The battle against sin begins in the mind. So decide you will put God first and give your very best to Him. Remember you are a child of God. As your mind goes, the man or woman follows. We become what we think. We do what we believe. Remember that God is for you, God is with you, and God is in you.

Repenting of your sins keeps us on the road to constant spiritual growth. Confession of wrongdoing and turning to God deepens the relationship you have with Him. You also then become more like Christ every day. It is an ongoing process of giving yourself to God.

Sometimes we are afraid to completely surrender our lives to God. This is a big mistake.

When we repent, we return to the power and direction of God. We give up our self-will. We stop trying to determine who we are without God. We stop feeling awkward, and we no longer resist giving control to God. God is forming us according to His master plan. God really knows what's best for us. He may want you to slow down, keep on your current road, speed up, stop, or completely change direction (turn left or turn right). We are to respond to His lead wherever it takes us. We want to walk with God.

You want God to give you what He knows is best for you. Trust Him to keep working on something better for us even when our prayers aren't

---

[9] Anonymous preaching elder, Worldwide Church of God, Baltimore,MD..

answered the way we want. Totally trusting God and loving people is the way to become content.

In this way, you will not develop a big head and think you did everything on your own. You recognize God is part of your life and knows what's best. You will not be wise in your own mind. You will not think more highly of yourself than you should.

Don't accept all the praise from others as they shower it on you. People may say that you did everything on your own. You know better. This is a test. Rather, give the credit and glory to God. Don't honor yourself. Turn the attention back to God. He did it through you.

True repentance is a gift from God. Allow yourself to be led and guided by the Holy Spirit.

A. The Humble Follower of Christ Walks as Holy Spirit Leads

Recognize you need to repent of your sins daily. You still have carnal human nature. Thank God for the help He gives you. You will refocus quickly after you have repented.

Jesus set the perfect example of humility. He knew from where He came. He was made fully human. He submitted to the flesh to become a servant. Allowing Himself to become like us, He suffered obedience unto death. He even died on the cross for us. Because He was fully divine, His death was special. He paid for the sins of the entire world—past, present, and future (Hebrews 2:9–12 NLT).

God wants you to be humble toward others as well (1 Peter 5:5–6 NKJV). Relating to our fellow man is often a challenge. When misfortune shows up, you will learn to do things differently—loving instead of hating, expressing kindness when you are accused, being gentle when others are harsh, and maintaining self-control when temptation strikes.

Value others more than yourself (Philippians 2:3–5). This is what Jesus Christ did.

Be a real servant to Jesus by making yourself available to serve others. Serving is not what we do for God but what He does through us. God is the one who determines how we are to serve Him. Servants follow instructions rather than choose what to do for their Master. "We are His workmanship, created in Christ Jesus for good works, which God prepared beforehand" (Ephesians 2:10 NASB). Our responsibility is to discover how He wants us to serve Him and then get busy doing those specific tasks. He's given us spiritual gifts that enable us to do exactly what He's planned for each of us (1 Corinthians 12:7). Also, no matter what we are doing, we are ultimately serving Christ. He wants you to work hard and do your best job. In addition, you must realize you cannot serve yourself and God at the same time. We have to overcome our self-centeredness. Jesus came not to be served but to serve. You must strive to be like Him. It is costly. It can be inconvenient and exhausting. Sometimes we feel limited by our health, financial resources, abilities, or age. Our attitude of love and desire to honor the Lord helps us see the opportunities God puts right in our path.

Walk humbly before God. Yield and submit yourself to Him. God rejoices when you repent.

A humble person is a praying person. You know you need God to make it.

God grants many blessings. First, you pray to God with more compassion and realness. You confirm He is most worthy, holy, righteous, and loving. You tell God you need Him. You are asking Him to lead and guide you today. Then you obey God quicker and in the way He requests. When He directs you toward something out of your comfort zone or another thing that you don't fully understand, you must still obey God since that is all you care about.

You realize you are in God's presence. God pays attention to you. "The high and lofty one who lives in eternity, the Holy One, says this: 'I live in the high and holy place with those whose spirits are contrite and humble.

I restore the crushed spirit of the humble and revive the courage of those with repentant hearts'" (Isaiah 57:15 NLT).

You are given more wisdom. Your prayers are heard (Psalm 10:7). Grace is given to you (James 4:6–7). You are exalted by God in the right way and right time.

Pride blocks humility. Remember all you have belongs to God. Offset the self by appreciating others. If you have a lot of possessions and/or money, give to the needy. If you have power and position, volunteer as a greeter or guide people to open parking. If you look great, get over yourself. Appreciate others who are trying to make it in the world. If you have great knowledge, learn to listen to others. Let others express their opinions. Encourage others. Compliment others. If you have achieved a lot, first point to God and then to others who helped you. If you are blessed with several talents and gifts, find a way to help others. Remember where your gifts came from—the Holy Spirit. The more skillful you are, the more careful you must be to protect yourself from becoming prideful. Ask a friend to tell you when vanity rears its ugly head. Pray to God to keep pride from becoming a hindrance to your growth and service. Pride has no place in God's kingdom.

Cultivate humility and keep growing. You must discard your own plans and desires for what God has planned for you. Keep asking, "What do You want to do through me? Your will be done." Worship the Father in Spirit and in truth (John 4:23–24 NLT).

I'm just like any carnal human. The nature of the flesh is governed by human nature. We tend to "gratify the desires of the flesh" or do "what your sinful nature craves" (Galatians 5:16–21; Colossians 3:5, 8). I, too, make bad decisions, resist obeying, and become bigheaded, hardheaded, and selfish at times.

But God wants us to let the Spirit guide our lives. He wants us to walk by the Spirit. Then we won't do what our sinful nature typically craves. "Do not let sin control the way you live; do not give in to sinful desires. Do not let any part of your body become an instrument of evil to serve sin.

Instead, give yourselves completely to God, for you were dead, but now you have new life. So use your whole body as an instrument to do what is right for the glory of God" (Romans 6:12, 13 NLT).

Despite our shortcomings, God has brought you and me where we're now. We are still works in progress. We are not yet at the place we need to be. God still watches over us with His love, compassion, and kindness. In this life as a fleshly human, my purpose for living is tied to Jesus Christ. I seek to do what He wants of me. He wants us to respect and revere Him. He wants me to walk in His ways.

There are several attitudes that can cause us to go the wrong way. Ask yourself these questions. Do you show vanity? Are you impatient with other people? Do you put on false airs? Are you snobbish, stuffy, or high-minded toward others? Are you considerate of all people? Do you exalt yourself? Do you compare yourself with others? Do you need to get rid of jealousy, resentment, and rudeness? Do you pick at other people? Do you judge others? If you commit any of these sins, you need repentance. Keep burying your old self and keep putting on the new self. Let the Holy Spirit guide you more and more. God tells us to come to Him and repent when we realize our mistakes. Admit your shortcomings and weakness. He is ready to forgive. This is how you keep that close relationship with God. This is how we fellowship with Him more and more.

Jesus wants us to be humble like little children. When the disciples asked Jesus, "Who then is the greatest in the kingdom of heaven?" He had a child stand in the middle of them. Children are lowly, weak, defenseless, and vulnerable. They are fully dependent on their parents. We are also fully dependent on God's mercy, kindness, and provision to us. We lean on God for eternal life. Salvation is given by grace, faith, and Jesus alone. Humility is a character trait that God values. Keep a broken and contrite heart, and offer God your spiritual sacrifice.

4. Submit to Those in Authority Over You

"Therefore, by Him let us continually offer the sacrifice of praise to God, that is, the fruit of our lips, giving thanks to His name. But do not forget to do good and share, for with such sacrifices God is well pleased. Obey those who rule over you, and be submissive, for they watch out for your souls, as those who must give account. Let them do so with joy and not with grief, for that would be unprofitable" (Hebrews 13:15–17 NKJV).

Romans 13:1–7 (NLT) says,

> "Everyone must submit to governing authorities. For all authority comes from God, and those in positions of authority have been placed there by God. So anyone who rebels against authority is rebelling against what God has instituted, and they will be punished. For the authorities do not strike fear in people who are doing right, but in those who are doing wrong. Would you like to live without fear of authorities? Do what is right, and they will honor you. The authorities are God's servants, sent for your good. But if you are doing wrong, of course you should be afraid,

for they have the power to punish you. They are God's servants, sent for the very purpose of punishing those who do what is wrong. So you must submit to them, not only to avoid punishment, but also to keep a clear conscience. Pay your taxes, too, for these same reasons. For government workers need to be paid. They are serving God in what they do. Give to everyone what you owe them, and give respect and honor to those who are in authority".

Everyone must submit to those who have authority over them. That includes the governmental authorities, family heads, church leaders, and bosses at work.

First, God has set up and formed governments. He determines who goes into office. He can set them up and take them down. There is no authority except from God. Those who serve the public are established by God. When things are going right, leaders are sent to punish those who do wrong and commend those who do right. He holds all those in authority accountable. God wants us to submit to governmental authority (1 Timothy 2:1–3 NLT). God watches over earthly affairs. He uses the world powers to complete His will. He has mercy on whomever He wants, and He hardens whomever He wants (Romans 9:18).

Be concerned about your leaders. There is a lot of talk between the United States and North Korea about the threat of nuclear confrontation. People are worried. They face hard choices and difficulties. They need wisdom and understanding to handle these crises.

Government is intended to be a servant to its citizens. When disaster strikes, government workers are concerned with your health and safety. Hurricane Harvey devastated Houston with record-breaking floodwaters in August 2017. Congress passed a bill to provide millions of dollars. President Trump visited Houston and Florida to pledge governmental support. FEMA did a lot. The mayor and various agencies encouraged police officers, hospital staff, military agencies, churches, businesses, and individuals to help countless victims. Hurricane Irma also hit Florida in August 2017, requiring much of the same aid. Maria hit Puerto Rico very hard as well. Government authorities were tested to creatively solve the problems at hand. The number of fatalities was low because people acted out of that sense of duty, concern, and love. You know God was in the middle of the effort. Great effort was made to rescue and evacuate residents. This is government at its best.

Support your leaders out of respect for them and God. Treat people with dignity. We should desire their highest good.

Pray for your leaders. The Bible commands us to pray for all those in leadership over us. Give prayers, petitions, and thanksgiving … for kings and all those in authority so that we may lead tranquil and quiet lives with godliness and thanksgiving (1 Timothy 2:1–2 NKJV). That includes men and women in public office—the presidency, congress, governor, mayor. Pray for their salvation, for their ability to lead or govern, and for their commitment to the highest standards and priorities. This is personal and professional. God works everything to its proper end (Proverbs 16:4). We know our leaders need God's help and direction. We want them to make the necessary changes in their lives. This is good and acceptable in the sight God, our Savior.

Live productive lives as responsible citizens (1 Peter 2:9 NJKV). Others should see your good example and notice God's involvement. Be a good citizen. Speak the truth. Your neighbor should trust you. Don't swear. "God works everything to its proper end. Endure and pray for the leaders. Live by faith, not by sight"[10]

Stay out of trouble. Obey the laws of the national, state, and local governments. Tell the truth, and be honest with others. If you are arrested, don't resist arrest. That means you should drive within the speed limit. That means you should not text while you are driving. That means you should buckle your seat belt. That means you should keep your license, permit, and current insurance in the vehicle. If you disagree with the

---

[10] Cedric Moore Preacher, "Live a Godly Life in spite of Living in an Ungodly World," Faith Community Shreveport, LA, April 19, 2015.

police, let the court decide. Be a good citizen. Seek to live godly lives in an ungodly world.

For the sake of your conscience, submit to God (Romans 13:5). Let the Holy Spirit prompt you to do good deeds. Pay your taxes. For God's sake, submit yourself to Him. Clothe yourself with Jesus Christ. Don't rebel.

Our ultimate leader is Jesus Christ. We need to honor God and Christ as our heavenly leader. We must walk in righteousness. Remain focused so that you stay free from sinful behavior, motives, and thoughts (Romans 13:13 –14).

With love, serve as a follower in Christ. We are citizens of the kingdom of God. God wants you to love Him and others. This all glorifies God. Therefore, trust your governing authorities.

Second, your family should adhere to a proper order of authority within the home. Colossians 3:18–21 says,

> "Children be praying for their parents; parents for their children; wives for their husbands; husbands for their wives. This is all part of how God works within a family both to bless its individual members and to make it a force of kingdom influence. Families operate best when following God's design: "Wives, be subject to your husbands, as is fitting in the Lord. Husbands, love your wives and do not be embittered against them. Children, be obedient to your parents in all things, for this is well-pleasing to the Lord. Fathers, do not exasperate your children, so they will not lose heart. The proper ordering of authority within the home, combined with prayer for one another, strengthens every ligament of relationship while leading each person to see themselves as ultimately submitted to the Lord. Caring and helping one another. Praying for one another. All out of obedience to Him.

Parents have a lot of experience and wisdom to share.

Third, church leaders should receive the same concerns and awareness that is given to governmental authorities. They are there to serve you. Submit yourself to your elders. They are responsible for guiding us so that we can mature and attain the fullness of Christ. Our leaders desire us to express love and humility toward one another. Our love and support is meant to give them joy in their work, which in turn blesses the entire church. Members can stay focused on their true calling. Pastors and other members of leadership enlighten us so that we can use the gifts we are given to help one another grow and become like Jesus. "God opposes the proud but shows favor to the humble" (1 Peter 5:5–7 NLT).

Fourth, your supervisors at work need your dedication and support as well. They want you to use your talents and abilities to provide quality products to the public. They are responsible for their employees too, and they should advocate for benefits including (1) providing direction, instruction, and examples to follow; (2) protecting with boundaries and rules; (3) praising those who do right; (4) punishing those who do wrong; and (5) pointing others to Christ. Any leader who dedicates him or herself to God can be used as a force of spiritual change for individuals and the entire culture at large. Laborers, submit to those who are good and considerate but also to those who are harsh. God wants you to work with zeal and solve problems in creative ways.[11], [12]

Employees, know and respect your limitations. Follow the line of authority. Don't go over your immediate supervisor's head until you have presented your case to him. Notify the right person when the solution to a problem is beyond your responsibility or ability.

If you are a person in a position of leadership and authority, you can always ask for the help with a proper attitude for those under your care. When you know how to talk to people, they will receive your instructions with open hearts and minds.

---

[11] Pastor Charles Stanley, *Handle with Care* (Colorado Springs, CO: David C. Cook Publisher, 2011), 113–16.
[12] Stephen and Alex Kendrick, *The Battle Plan for Prayer* (Nashville: B & H Publishing Group, 2015), 206–10, 237.

We all have to answer to somebody, even if you own your own business. There are deadlines to meet. There are regulations to respect. There are resources to obtain and use. You are dealing with people during all these processes.

"Remind them to be subject to rulers, to authorities, to be obedient, to be ready for every good deed, to malign no one, to be peaceable, gentle, showing every consideration for all men" (Titus 3:1–2 NASB).

The Message version of the Bible says, "Remind the people to respect the government and be law abiding, always ready to lend a helping hand. No insults, no fights, God's people should be bighearted and courteous." You can see God wants us to set good examples along with those who have authority over us. He knows this is challenging. You will have to stay close to Him to pull it off.

Remember you are living for God and His spirit is in you.

When you submit to those who have authority over you, you offer a spiritual sacrifice.

Here is an outstanding prayer about living under authority.

> "Father, I acknowledge that all authority is from You and that all my authorities only have power because of You. I choose to pray for the biblical, governmental, family, and employment authorities You have placed over my life as a demonstration of my submission to You. Please draw them to salvation and give them a fear of the Lord in all their decisions. Use them to guide, protect, praise and discipline me in order that I might do Your will, even as I do the same for those under my authority. Use me to be a blessing; Grant me favor so I can daily help people live out their full potential under Your total authority and lordship."[13]

---

[13] Stephen and Alex Kendrick, *The Battle Plan for Prayer* (Nashville: B & H Publishers, 2015), 210.

PART TWO – THE LEGS

Walk in the Direction of Right, Light, and Truth

The legs show one's walk and actual conduct. We are to walk God's way after the Spirit and in faith. People aren't able to direct their steps correctly. We must desire to walk in God's way. We are to walk in a manner worthy of the Lord in order to please Him in every area of our lives. Jesus is the only way to God the Father (John 14: 6). We should set our hearts on becoming more like Christ. Delight in this way. Walk in the way that the Lord has commanded you. Let God direct your steps. You will have a long life. So if you are going toward Jesus Christ, you are going the Way. God wants to be involved in every area of our lives. Peter told the listeners the first step. We are to repent and be baptized for the forgiveness of your sins. Then you will receive the gift of the Holy Spirit (Acts 2:38). The Holy Spirit will then instruct us in the way of Jesus. The Holy Spirit will guide us in our shared walk as Christians in the way. The Holy Spirit gives the desire and ability to walk in obedience to His will. This leads to eternal life. Keep asking God to help you remain on the narrow road that leads to Jesus Christ and eternal life. This includes walking in the light and the truth.

5. Keep Praying with Great Confidence

"May my prayer be set before you like incense; may the lifting up of my hands be like the evening sacrifice" (Psalm 141:2).

Prayer is an act of worship. In the Old Testament, much of the worship carried out by God's people was related to the sacrificial system set down by God's law. These sacrificial acts of the worshippers were associated with and accompanied by praying and making an entreaty to God. As the aromas of the sacrifices went up from the altar, prayers also ascended to God. As New Testament worshippers, we don't kill and burn animals or offer incense as sacrifices to the Lord. God calls us to offer up a different kind of sacrifice—that of personal prayer. We are to lift our prayers to Him. We are to offer the incense of our prayers. And unlike the Old Testament worshippers, we can offer up our sacrifices of prayer anywhere and at any time.

In prayer we offer the sacrifice of forgiveness. While dedicating himself to the temple, King Solomon also indicated that prayer and repentance was the way to obtain forgiveness from God (1 Kings 8:46–50).

Praying is simply talking to Father God. This is a personal and private affair. He wants you to take the time to tell Him you love Him and that you need Him. Conversing with God is about telling Him all your thoughts, concerns, dreams, needs, and wants. Tell Him what is important to you, whether it's small or large. This shows you are assured that He is listening. You know you can talk to Him in a few seconds, minutes, or hours. You may say just a few words or a phrase, or you may just have a thought. You know you can talk to God about anything. Talk to God from the heart. We are His children. So make your needs known to Him. Let's draw near to Him and enjoy His presence.

God wants you to pray from your heart and really mean it. He requires that you be truthful and honest with Him. Share with God your specific concerns in a humble way. You know He loves you and always does what's best for you. So tell Him what's on your mind and heart. Be yourself.

Keep prayer as your priority. This is how you solve problems when you present them to God directly and personally. This is how you keep the close relationship growing. This is how you remove the depression, anxiety, worry, and fear. This is how He brings out the truth. This is how you know what God wants you to do today. This is how spiritual battles are won in the end. This is how your relationship grows stronger.

Prayer is the most powerful weapon available to you. After putting on the armor of God for spiritual battle, God then tells us to pray in all occasions. Keep praying for God's involvement and direction in your life (Ephesians 6:18).

Bible study and prayer are so closely linked. As you study the Word of God, you learn about Him and yourself. You better realize God has a master plan for you, the church, and the world. It's His will that you inherit eternal life through Jesus Christ. You realize God is in control and is leading and guiding you toward that goal. The Bible tells you what He is doing and how you must live in response. Thus, you know what to pray about. You know you are a fleshly being that needs Jesus. You know God will provide what you need. He will teach you, rebuke you, correct you, and train you for righteousness. So you know you will succeed if you make adjustments in your life every day. Realize all you have to do is ask God for understanding and wisdom to follow His lead. In His Word, He gives many examples about how to pray, what to pray for, and who to pray for.

You know God will answer your prayer at the best time and in the best way. He knows what is best for you because of His love for you. Thus, you can always pray with confidence.

Your prayer life reflects how intimate your relationship is with your Father. Keep taking the time and effort. This is how we keep in contact with Him. Friends talk to one another often. Jesus called us His friends. This is a major way that our relationship deepens. Look forward to your one-on-one talk with God. He looks forward to that after all.

Even though the Father knows what your needs and wishes are, you still must ask Him for help and guidance. Of course, after asking, leave it in His hands. No matter what you need (little or big), ask Him. There are unlimited reasons to talk to God on a personal level.

Prayer is your first and lasting line of communication with Him. He expects you to talk to Him every day in various situations. Your relationship is strengthened as you talk to God. Cry out to God in your trouble. Let Him know you need Him.

In this way, you can show God that you really trust, have faith, and have total confidence in Him. You trust that God knows what is best for you. You know God has the desire and power to do what is best for you. You have faith in the faithfulness of God. He keeps His promises every time.

God wants you to begin your prayer with praise and thanksgiving. This shows you know He is awesome, powerful, and loving. Does God's grace and mercy move you beyond thanksgiving to swearing allegiance to Him and the kingdom of God? This is what Daniel did when he asked God to reveal a dream and the meaning of a king (Daniel 2:19–23). The more time you spend with God, the deeper you recognize how wise and dedicated He is to your present and the future.

You can use the model prayer as a guide. Jesus gave us the best foundational prayer to follow (Matthew 6:8–15 NKJV). As you know, there are many outstanding prayers in the Holy Bible that serve as our examples. Elijah and Jehoshaphat are good examples of praying with authority in deep humility. You must agree with God about who you are and what you cannot do (2 Chronicles 20:6–12). They were human just as we are. You can move mountains (problems or hard times) by claiming the authority of Jesus Christ.

The real key is to pray according to God's will. To know His will, we must know His thoughts. To know His thoughts, we must saturate our minds with His Word. You'll know His ways and His love for you. We then begin to partake of the authority of God in our prayers. Then we can rebuke the enemy and bind him from our thoughts. The essence of spiritual warfare is binding. You are in warfare with your enemy, the devil. Claim the cross of Jesus. The apostle Paul tells us to resist the evil one. Stand firmly on the truth of God. We are commanded to fight.

We are to bring things under the rule of Jesus on purpose. By dedicating yourself—or your home, relationship, job, among other things—you have brought what you have under Jesus's rule and authority.

God does answer prayers in His own way and time. We are to keep asking and requesting. The answer will come when God is ready and you are prepared for the answer. You know God's character, passion, and promises will work out for you. Keep asking, and patiently wait for God to act. If there is something He wants you to do, He'll tell you. God wants you to pray, wait, and act on the answer.

We have been given the authority of Jesus to use in prayer. We do this in Jesus's name. Present your request to God in the form of a petition, or make an intercession on behalf of others. Request deliverance from your problem. Confess your sins to God. End your prayer by saying, "In the name of Jesus."

"The effective prayer of a righteous man accomplishes much" (James 5:16b). The whole person—life, heart, and mind—should practice praying.

It takes a whole heart for effectual prayer. You must keep at it until God answers you.

Keep talking to God in your mind. Keep talking to God about anything and everything, whether big or small. Keep asking for wisdom and guidance. Just keep talking to God.

Keep your confidence strong. God will answer at the right time and in the best way.

A. Pray for Others

God does not want you to talk just about your needs, concerns, and wants. Of course, there are times when you must ask for direct help right then. There are times when you must make a special request to God on your behalf. However, the bulk of your time and focus should include others as you make intercessions. Show your concern and love for others by praying for them. You will need to intercede for them and/or offer a petition for them at times.

We want to see God meet the needs and make the necessary changes in their lives. Be as specific as you can be about each person's life and challenges. Love and compassion must fill our hearts when we pray.

You are the link between God's unlimited resources and people's needs. Identify with the needs of the people. Feel what they feel. See what they see. When we suffer hurt, we have a better chance to understand what they are going through. Then our prayer is more meaningful. Seek what's best for the person. God knows what that is. Don't give up praying for the person. Ask God what you can do for those you are praying for. Ask God to open your eyes to the needs of those around you. Get very specific.

In *The Battle Plan for Prayer*, Stephen and Alex Kendrick provide an outstanding strategy of praying for others. Here are some people you can pray for. You can focus on two or more groups at a time. But you should try to include them all before the week is over.

1. **Praying for Your Wife (or Yourself)**

   Ask God so that you can grow in love, support, submission, and respect. She needs to love the Lord with all her heart, mind, soul, and strength. Help her find her beauty and identity in Christ and reflect His character. Enable her to be patient, kind, hard to offend, and quick to forgive. Pray that her sexual needs are met only by her husband and that she meets his. Pray that she has her own career and feels a sense of accomplishment. Give her common sense and financial intelligence. Guide her so that she and her children act responsible and full of respect.

2. **Praying for Your Husband (or Yourself)**

   Ask God to enable him to truly love and protect you (his wife). Pray that he will love the Lord with all his heart, mind, soul, and strength. Help him serve as a hard worker and remain responsible. Enable him to provide for his family. Ask that he knows God and seeks to do His will. He should be a strong spiritual leader with courage, wisdom, and conviction. Give him good common sense and the desire to do right. Help him to depend on God more than himself. Reading the Word of God will guide his decisions and judgment. Help him to be patient, kind, hard to offend, and quick to forgive. Pray that he meets your sexual needs and that he meets yours.

3. **Praying for Your Children**

   It would be great if they came to know Christ early in life. Ask for protection from evil in each area of their lives—spiritually, emotionally, mentally, and physically. Pray that they respect and submit to those in authority. Ask that they be surrounded by the right kind of friends and avoid the wrong friends. Pray that they love the Lord with their hearts, minds, souls, and strength. Ask God to guide them to make right decisions regarding their educational choices, marriages, job options, friendships, and spiritual moments.

4. **Praying for Your Pastor or Minister at Your Church**

Help him correctly divide the Word and clearly communicate the gospel. Place in his heart the desire to reach out to the lost and to be an effective and fruitful winner of souls. Guide him to keep his priorities in line with the will of God. Ask that he stay close to God. Ask that he has the courage to go in new directions to expand the gospel to others. Ask him to be an effective teacher of the truth of God.

5. **Praying for Governmental Authorities/Boss at Work over You/ Coworkers**

Pray for their salvation and their ability to lead and govern rightly. Encourage them to lead with honor, respect, wisdom, compassion, and godliness. Ask for their commitment to the highest standards and priorities. This is a commitment in both a personal and professional sense. Ask that they would use good judgment, seek justice, love mercy, and walk humbly with God. It's also good to pray for your bosses and managers at work. Ask God to provide direction, instruction, and good examples to follow. Ask that He offer protection with boundaries and rules, praise those who do right, and punish those who do wrong. Your coworkers should be a part of your prayer request. Here is a prayer for equality at the workplace from "My Daily Devotion" on a morning in September 2017.

> "Mighty Jesus, I pray for equality at my workplace. May You grant my employers and [collegium] the spirit of fairness and justice. O Lord, help us to interact with others freely regardless of our experiences, skills, qualifications, or ranks at our workplace. Guide us to share ideas for growth of our organization, individual experience, and for the glory of Your holy name. Help us, O Lord, to appreciate one another, and grant us the gift of love in everything. We do it through the

name of Your holy Son, Jesus Christ. We pray trusting and believing in You. Amen."[14]

6. Praying for Those Who Don't Know Christ

Pray regularly for those lost in nations around the world. There are millions of people who still need to hear the greatest news in the world—the gospel. Ask for God's Spirit to convict them of sin, God's coming judgment, and their need for a Savior. Ask that they be granted repentant hearts that turn fully to Christ (Colossians 4:2–4). Ask that their eyes be opened so that they see how badly they need the Savior, Jesus Christ. Tell them about His love and forgiveness. Through your gentle, patient, and clear testimony, ask that nonbelievers see Jesus. Your lifestyle should encourage them to seek God. Then grant them repentance that leads to knowledge of the truth. We want them to come to their senses and escape the snare of the devil.

7. Praying for Other Believers

Pray for those believers who are being persecuted for their love and service to Jesus. Ask for believers to desire more spiritual truth. It is time for a revival. Thank God for them. Encourage them. Bring their concerns before the Lord. Ask that the world see God's power and see the difference He makes in our lives.

8. Praying for Laborers in the Harvest (Luke 10:2)

Various groups are taking God's Word to the least, last, and lost around them. Pray that they will be strong in the Lord (1 Corinthians 15:58 NKJV). Ask God to keep opening doors for the gospel. Ask to send laborers to the community serving in this way. Ask that the Holy Spirit be poured out in revival. We want to honor God.

---

[14] "My Daily Devotions," September 2017.

9. Praying for Your City

The views of top leaders and elected officials views are often different from ours, but God can turn the hearts of rulers. He can provide us with godly leaders who want to serve wisely and justly. He can strengthen law enforcement to truly protect people and get rid of crime. Raise up strong pastors and healthy churches.[15]

Take each one, and list your concerns. Again, be as specific as you can be.

"Abba, Father today I just want to thank and praise you, for being my God, my King and my Savior. I know my life would have been nothing without you. I thank you for the relationship I have with you my Lord. You are everything to me, and I am not ashamed or afraid to talk of your goodness. Help me to stand up for the truth, and share the gospel with others. For many do not understand the purpose of our lives, and this life is not just about us. The purpose of our lives is to share the gospel, love and care for our fellow brothers and sisters, and live a God fearing life. For this is just temporary. Yes Father, we all love good things. But we must not put them first in our lives, but put you first. Father God as I bow in your presence this morning, I bring each and every one of us before you. Forgive us this morning if we have sinned against you in any way at all. We are sorry Lord, cleanse us, and help us to better people. And also, help us bring more people into the Kingdom of God. For that is our purpose Lord. We also ask in your mighty hand of healing, grace, and blessing to be upon us. Amen." ("Angel," *139 Daily Devotions*)[16]

As you pray to God about everything, keep offering your spiritual sacrifice. Prayer pleases God. So keep on talking with confidence. You know He will answer you (Proverbs 15:8).

---

[15] Stephen and Alex Kendrick, *The Battle Plan for Prayer* (Nashville: H & B Publishing Group), 232–41.
[16] "Angel," *139 Daily Devotions*.

6. Do What's Just and Right

Practice Justice and Righteousness

"Even though you offer up to Me burnt offerings and your grain offerings, I will not accept them And I will not even look at the peace offerings of your fatlings. Take away from Me the noise of your songs; I will not even listen to the sound of your harps. But let justice roll down like waters and righteousness like even flowing stream" (Amos 5:22–24 NASB).

"Thus says the LORD, 'Do justice and righteousness, and deliver the one who has been robbed from the power of his oppressor. Also do not mistreat or do violence to the stranger, the orphan, or the widow; and do not shed innocent blood in this place'" (Jeremiah 22:3 NASB).

"The LORD is more pleased when we do what is right and just, than when we offer him sacrifices" (Proverbs 21:3 NLT).

"Trust (lean on, rely on, and be confident) in the Lord and do good; so shall you dwell in the land and feel surely on His faithfulness, and truly you shall be fed" (Psalm 36:3 AMPC).

God is in the habit of telling us to be like Him. God is righteous and deals with us through justice. He tells us to be holy because He is holy. He wants to see righteousness in us through Jesus. He wants us to love Him and our fellow man since He is love. So He wants us to love Him and people. He wants us to be just and right in our dealing with others as He walks (Proverbs 8:20). One of the reasons that God inspired the book of Proverbs was to help us do what is right, just, and fair toward one another (Proverbs 1:3b; 3:9).

After King Nebuchadnezzar was humbled by God, he said, "I … praise and exult, and glorify the King of heaven, *because everything he does is right and all his ways are just.* And those who walk in pride he is able to humble" (Daniel 4:37). God wants us to treat our fellow man justly and to do what's right according to His standards. This is part of His very character and nature. This is who He really is. He wants us to be like Him.

God expects this kind of conduct no matter what the person's culture, race, religion, economic standing, or background may be. Everyone is a human being and created in God's image. Love everybody regardless of what kind of title they have or don't have. Don't boast about things you have or don't have. Just be quite about these. Don't ridicule people. God will work it out. God expects this kind of behavior even when it involves your enemy. You may dislike a certain thing that people do, but don't hate them. Of course, God is there to help you. Do good rather than evil. Pray for your enemies, and you will be blessed.

To care about other people means you are discarding your selfish nature more and more. True and active love becomes your life theme. You will decide to fill your mind more with thoughts that make you kind, loving, and generous to others. You will have to face some unpleasant truths about yourself. I grew up in a family of twelve. Of course, I wanted to survive. I didn't always tell the truth, but I always had food to eat and clothes on my back. I knew I was loved. I enjoy being in my family. I never knew I was poor until someone told me. I am rich in the love I experience with my family. I wasn't a people person at first. I am learning to do better. I don't like to talk a lot unless I am asked specific questions. I would rather talk one-on-one with a person. I learned to listen and keep secrets. But I didn't think about other people who may be in need. I was used to working alone. Studying in college and working in my classroom as a teacher caused me to think only about what I needed to do for my students. One of my sisters needed a place to store some furniture for a month so that she could get a new apartment. My mom suggested she stay with me. I was glad to help my sister. At age twenty-one, it never occurred to me that I could help others like that. When I finally talk to people, I better understood what they are like. Then I hope the best for them. When I got away from thinking only about myself, I was able to pray for others and wish the best for them or actually do something to help them.

Be kind to the oppressed. Have compassion for them. Treat others the way you want to be treated. This is the golden rule. Treat others with respect by not looking down on them. Loving others unconditionally is hard work. It takes the power of the Holy Spirit to do it right and consistently. Opportunities come up in simple ways every day.

Don't mistreat or oppress others. Rather be kind to them. Through Moses, God tells Israel to do right by their fellow man. The same applies to modern-day Christians. Therefore, do not steal, lie, deceive, defraud, rob, use perverse justice, spread slander, hate, bear a grudge, take revenge, or hold on to a person's wages to Saturday (Leviticus 19:11–18). Rather God wants us to love our neighbors as ourselves. He wants us to relate to one another in positive ways.

Be fair by treating everyone the same. Do not treat people differently because of their race, color, national origin, sex, age, or disability. If you own a business, expect everyone to work hard. Give your employees more than minimum wages. Good work deserves good wages. Make sure you pay them on time too.

Seek to do good deeds when the opportunity arrives (Titus 3:8b, 14). When you have a chance to bless people and help them, do it. Here are a very few small ways you can make a difference in people's lives.

- Open or hold the door for someone.

- Give credit to the person who deserves it so that others can hear it.
- Sponsor a trip for teenager going on a church activity to a major city.
- Give a gift card to a deserving young person.
- Let people know you appreciate what they did for you.
- When you have a chance to help, speak positively, or reward people for their work.
- Give school supplies, tennis shoes, or school clothes to those needy persons.
- Help new coworkers understand their jobs better.
- Encourage a young person to keep going to school.
- Do a good thing just because someone deserves it.
- If people cooked a great meal, planned a great wedding, or repaired your car or appliance, thank them, and tell them you appreciate it very much.
- If you're in line and someone cuts in front of the person whose before you, speak up, and remind that new person that you and the other person were already here. Point and tell the mistaken person, "That's the end of the line."
- Give your money to the cashier even if he gets busy and doesn't ask for it. Give back the money when the cashier gives you more change than you're owed. Give back any extra money when a person overpays you.

This list can include so many other things you can do to show mercy and concern for others. Don't be afraid to venture out of your comfort zone.

Tell the truth all the time. Wisdom from God will help your words ring of truth. Tell the truth about your feelings, beliefs, and thoughts when asked. If you are an eyewitness, only tell the authorities what you actually saw or heard. People will better know what you really think. They will know your views and morals. You are a friend when you tell the truth. They will want your opinions and views after they know you always tell them the truth.

You avoid the many faces of lying. You don't slander, gossip, flatter, or exaggerate. You don't give half-truths. Rather you love the truth and live the truth. Your word is your bond. People can stand on your word.[17]

God expects you to be truthful. He wants you to be honest with yourself first. One of the things God hates is a lying tongue (Proverbs 6:17–19).

Do not wrong your brother or take advantage of him (1 Thessalonians 4:6).

Paul tells us to keep on loving one another as brothers. Then he said, "Remember those in prison as if you were their fellow prisoners, and those who are mistreated as if you yourselves were suffering" (Hebrews 13:3 NIV).

Share with others your gifts, fortune, and attitude of love. You'll be a magnet for good. In order for any of these actions to really take place, we must walk and live by the Spirit (Galatians 5:16, 22–26). Let the Spirit lead you and guide you. He will give you a renewed concern for others. He will open your eyes so that you can see spiritual matters better.

We will need to meet the needs of others around us. Ask God to show you how to meet the needs of those in your family, coworkers, and community members. You love God by loving your neighbors. Loving God and loving the people He has placed in your life should define your entire way of life.

The person who lives well, treats others fairly, and keeps good relationships with others is awarded a long and good life. In addition, if these people obey God's commands, God will grant them full and true lives. Look at the list of twelve practices these kind of people don't do to determine their fate (Ezekiel 18:5–9 The Message). As a goal, we should try to live well, treat others fairly, and keep good relationships with others.

God wants you to do what is good in regard to your fellow man. He wants you to be ready and eager to do good for others (Titus 2:14b; 3:1; 8:14b NIV).

---

[17] John Moore Preacher, "Tell the Truth," Faith Community in Shreveport, LA, May 28, 2017.

Every believer should be a living, walking example of good deeds. Faith, hope, and love should motivate us to do good. God determines what He wants each of us to do. Then He equips us for whatever He calls us to actually do. Jesus uses the unlimited resources He has to empower us to accomplish those good deeds. He uses the scripture to train us. He uses our brothers and sisters in Christ to motivate us to do good works. He can even use our money to help us become generous and ready to share. Next, we must remember we are to glorify God with those good works, not ourselves. God will one day judge our good works. Those good works will provide great rewards that exceed our imagination.

We who are strong in Christ and faith should do what we can for our spiritual brothers and sisters' good. There are four qualities God wants us to demonstrate. First, God wants us to bear with the failings of the weak. We must understand where they are in attitudes and abilities. Second, we should build others up according to their needs. When others are hurt or offended, Jesus was there to encourage them. We must say things that are enriching to them. Third, we should live in unity and harmony with one another. Bring who you are out, and offer service and kindness. Fourth, you should accept others just like Christ accepted you. Accept them just as they are, and don't try to make them into the way you want them (Romans 15:1–7 NIV). Be strong and graceful Christians.[18]

Be prepared to suffer for doing good. But you are blessed (1 Peter 3:8–12; 4:12–19).

God commands us to love our fellow humans (John 13:34; 15:12 NASB).

Be careful not to get tired of doing good. Everything will work out for you.

God wants us to simply do the right thing because it is the right thing to do.

"The LORD detests the way of the wicked but he loves those who pursue righteousness" (Proverbs 5:9b).

---

[18] Mike Booze Pastor, "Strong Graceful Christians," Faith Community, January 18, 2015.

The book of Proverbs has several purposes. "There purpose is to teach people to live disciplined and successful lives, to help them to do what's right, just, and fair" (Proverbs 1:3 NLT).

God wants you to doing good deeds with humility. Every time you choose to do good instead of sin, you are growing in the character of Christ. Every time you defeat a temptation, you become more like Jesus (James 3:13). Every time you do good for others, you offer a pleasing sacrifice to God.

"He has shown you, O mortal, what is good. And what does the LORD require of you? To act justly and to love mercy and to walk humbly with your God" (Micah 6:8).

In summary, seek ways to do what is just, right, and good to your fellow man. "So let's not allow ourselves to get fatigued doing good. At the right time we will harvest a good crop if we don't give up, or quit. Right now, therefore, every time we get the chance, let us work for the benefit of all, starting with the people closest to us in the community of faith" (Galatians 6:9–10 The Message).

7. Supply the Needs of Others

Philippians 4:15–18 (NLT) says,

> "As you know, you Philippians were the only ones who gave me financial help when I first brought you the Good News and then traveled on from Macedonia. No other church did this. Even when I was in Thessalonica you sent help more than once. I don't say this because I want a gift from you. Rather, I want you to receive a reward for your kindness. At the moment I have all I need … and more! I am generously supplied with gifts you sent me with Epaphroditus. They are a sweet-smelling sacrifice that is acceptable and pleasing to God."

The apostle Paul thanks the Philippian church for providing gifts of money, food, clothes, and other things when he was in need. They were very concerned for his needs. They saw and then provided whatever he needed. Paul told them that he had enough.

God wants you to also help people in need and those who are less fortunate. There are many ways to provide for others' needs beyond money. Share your gifts and talents with those who have need for them or with those whose lives you can make easier.

Take care of the needs of people in the name of Jesus. A mind-set for service makes this possible. When you see someone in need, take responsibility for that need. Check to see whether you have the ability to help. Do you have the character, maturity, time, and talent? Then get organized and move ahead. This is not easy to do. It will take intimacy with God, healing, favor, protection, wisdom, knowledge, discernment, creativity, gifts of the Spirit, productivity, and prudence (good management). Ask God for an increase in good health, energy, zeal, passion, enthusiasm, anointing, peace, enjoyment, laughter, giving, and hearing from Him. You are unique in your experiences and insight. He will provide what's needed. He sees you want to serve.

There are some ministries you are currently doing or have taken part in. There are so many ministries available to you. You just have to see the need and do what you can to meet that need. Check out *Meeting Needs, Sharing Christ* by Donald Atkinson and Charles Roesel.[19]

If you don't actually know what your gift is, take a survey online to find out. Answer the questions, and you'll get at least a partial awareness or a confirmation of your strengths, abilities, and interest. God has plans for you. Ask yourself the following questions: What do I love to do? What do I dream of doing? What fascinates me? What can I talk about, think about, and study all day long and not get bored with? Where have I been most effective in my life?

Filling a need may be just a small matter. The roll of paper towels may need to be refilled. You can start the dishwasher, unload the dryer, or cover up food just sitting out. You may sing well enough to join the choir's tenor or soprano section. You can cut the grass for an elderly person, loan a friend a tool, and serve as an extra pair of hands.

---

[19] Donald Atkins and Charles Roesel, *Meeting Needs, Sharing Christ* (Nashville: LifeWay Press, 1995), 81–93.

Be available for God to use you. Ask God what new thing you can do today. Ask Him what He wants you to learn today. Ask Him to help improve various areas of your life so that you can be helpful to others.

Be aware of small and big opportunities we have in God. After John the Baptist spoke honestly about our need for repentance, the crowd asked, "What shall we do then?" He basically told them to be generous with those who have nothing. Tax collectors were told to be honest, and some soldiers were told to be content (Luke 3:7–14). Thus, God wants you to be generous, honest, and content with what you have.

Ask God to help you provide for the needs of others. Thus, you must be willing to share and to put your compassion into action. God wants you to reach out and meet the needs of others by sharing your gifts and talents. Tabitha (Dorcas) was a disciple. She did good as she helped the poor. Then she died. Some of the needy showed others the clothes and robes she had made for the poor. (Her main service was sewing for the poor.) Through Peter, God raised her from the dead so she could continue to make an important contribution. God valued her seemingly small service. God values all acts of service small and great. He does not overlook or forget the small acts of kindness we do for others. Dorcas had the spiritual gift of mercy and service. She combined that with her talent for sewing in order to serve others. God notices every act of kindness, even giving a person a glass of water (Acts 9:32–43). Nothing you do for others escapes God's notice. All acts of kindness are valuable in the kingdom of God.

Becoming a kinder person will cost you something. You will have to sacrifice time, money, energy, reputation, privacy, or something. The Good Samaritan willingly gave up a lot. He helped an injured person without expecting anything back. He gave first aid at the scene, put him on a donkey, took him to a motel, cared for him through the night, and paid the bill. The Good Samaritan interrupted his own schedule to help a stranger. He dropped everything. He was also willing to take risks. So God wants us to extend love to those who are hurting (Luke 10:34b–35). This is an act of worship and honor to God.

The world is full of wounded people in the heart and mind. You may not be aware of many people who could use your concern and kindness. So ask God to make you more aware of those who need help.

Those who show kindness to others will be blessed. God meets your needs (Isaiah 58:10–11). Other people will want to be kind to you.

Sometimes you show kindness by sharing your food, clothes, water, and other things. God takes note of what you do. He rewards you mightily. "Then the King will say to those on the right, 'Come, you who are blessed by my Father, take your inheritance, the Kingdom prepared for you since the creation of the world.' Then the righteous will answer him, 'Lord, When did we see you hungry and feed you, or thirsty and give you something to drink? When did we see you a stranger and invite you in, or needing clothes and clothe you? When did we see you sick or in prison and go to visit you?' And the King will reply, "Truly I tell you, whatever you did for one of the least of these brothers and sisters of mine, you did for me."" As you help your fellow man, you are taking care of problems others have. You are showing kindness and a desire to serve (Matthew 25:34, 37–40). God is very pleased to see you doing this. Unknowingly, we serve the Lord by serving others.

Hurricane Harvey flooded east Texas (particularly Houston) in August 2017. The floodwaters got up to fifty-three inches in some places. It devastated homes and businesses. Some got out, but many did not. Fellow Texans helped one another during and after the hurricane.

A lot of people who used to live in Houston and the surrounding area came to help however they could. These people shared nonperishable goods, rescue time and effort, clothing, transportation, and their homes. Prayers were behind all of this. Money came in from different sources—churches, *Good Morning America*, news stations, foundations, and individuals. NFL players and team organizations did a lot too. J. J. Watt from the Texas NFL team motivated more than $17 million for relief. Kindness, love, and concern motivated people to do all of this. It is good to see people from all walks of life donate like this. People brought items by car and bus to some places that had been devastated. Then these items were distributed and given to the victims. God was in the middle of this, and He was pleased. He touched many hearts and minds as they sacrificed time, money, and items to help those in real need. I also made a donation. People also donated for the relief effort in the Florida Keys after Hurricane Irma. Puerto Rico was also badly damaged by a hurricane.

People may hurt beyond just physical ways. They may be wounded emotionally, financially, or spiritually. This means we have to be more aware when something is different. Sometimes you can pick up on their sadness, anxiety, concern, or cluelessness. The Holy Spirit will open your spiritual eyes so that you can see certain needs and figure out how to approach people. Let these individuals know that God is ready to help them. Don't wait until it's more convenient for you. Don't put off what you know you should do for people today. God will be right there as you seize the moment.

You are not saved by service, but you are saved for service to God (2 Timothy 1:9a TLB). By serving God, you honor Him. You serve out of joy and deep gratitude.

So ask yourself, "Who needs my help today? Who needs my prayers? Who needs my provision?" When you give of yourself, you have a great impact on others.

"And do not forget to do good and to share with others, for with such sacrifices God is pleased" (Hebrews 3:16).

Align Your Feelings, Desires, and Motivations with God

The inwards signifies one's deep feelings and affections of the heart. Your heart represents the source of all your emotions – what you love to do and what you care about most. Another word for heart is passion. Don't ignore your interests. Have mercy and compassion on others in need. Consider how your abilities and talents might be used for God's glory. Really getting to know God personally is the true purpose of life. We should actually crave, pursue, and go with all our might to find God. We are to seek God not just when we are in trouble and need help when we are at church, when it's convenient, or when we feel afraid or obligated. We are to seek and love God with all our heart with deep compassion (Matthew 22: 37).

God encourages us to love one another and enjoy helping them. Jesus was gracious, forgiving, and generous. He has unconditional love for us all. The greatest challenge is to get our mind off our self and spend our lives to see how much we can care for others (John 13:4). This is a choice we make about the way we treat people on purpose. Love moves us to take action.

We want to do what is right. "Let love be the main theme of your life and you will have a life worth living." God wants us to intentionally make a point to being a blessing to others around us. We can do good things for people in our daily lives- "people in your family, people you don't know, and those we think deserve good treatment as well as those you don't think deserve that."

Be ready for opportunities to help others in little and big ways. I would get my breakfast at the same carry-out store most mornings on my way to driving to work. Two ladies always cooked very well at a local all-purpose gas station. I stop there for breakfast three out of five days. So around the Christmas season, I gave them both some money. I told them I wanted to give them a little money because they worked hard all year, and I wanted to let them know I appreciated them. It was God who inspired me to do this. Another opportunity came as I was driving to and from work and home. I noticed a man needing some extra clothes (coat, shirts, and pants). I resisted at first. Then I gathered some old clothes, kept them in my truck, and finally gave them to him. He smiled in a big way. On another time, one day, I was heading home from work. I stopped at a store and was pulling out. A young girl (nineteen to twenty-one)wearing a McDonald uniform asked me for a ride to get some transfer papers. She had to walk five to seven miles to and from work. Plus, it was getting dark on this road. At first, I said no. God convicted me as she started walking. I then turned around and waved to her. I could see that walk was going to take a lot out of her. So after I drove her to work and back to the area where I picked her up, I gave her some money. She thanked me and she praised God with feeling. God brought me to that spot at that time for this reason.

8. Praise God Continually

"Through Him then, let us continually offer up a sacrifice of praise to God, that is, the fruit of lips that give thanks to His name" (Hebrew 13:15 NASB).

"I will praise the LORD at all times; I will constantly speak his praises" (Psalm 34:1 NLT).

"I will exult you, my God and King, and praise your name forever and ever. I will praise you every day; yes, I praise you forever. Great is the LORD! He is most worthy of praise! No one can measure his greatness Let each generation tell its children of your mighty acts; let them proclaim your power" (Psalm 145:1–4 NLT).

"Take words with you, And return to the LORD, Say to Him, Take away all iniquity; Receive us graciously, For we offer the sacrifice of our lips" (Hosea 14:2 NKJV).

"Praise the LORD, you his servants; praise the name of the LORD. Let the name of the LORD be praised, both now and forever" (Psalm 113:1–2).

You should always praise God. This should be the first thing we do when seek God's audience. The angels of God always give praise at His throne. They see the wonderful things He does. It's been millions of years, and they are continuously amazed and thrilled. They can't stop giving Him praise. Nor should we!

God made us to give praise to Him. "The people I formed for myself that they may proclaim my praise" (Isaiah 43:21). "But you are a chosen people, a royal priesthood, a holy nation, God's special possession, that you may declare the praises of him who called you out of darkness into his wonderful light" (1 Peter 2:9). You are meant to praise God.

Praising God enables us to enter His very presence with gladness and confidence. You can talk to Him from a humble mind and heart about anything. You recognize He has great power, wisdom, and unlimited love. It's like comparing a newborn baby to a college professor. You see how little you are. It is easy to let Him know how much He is in comparison to you. Your problem is so little compared to His greatness. You shift from focusing on yourself to focusing on God.

Scripture demands that you praise God as you recognize who He really is. Moses said, "He is my God and I will praise Him" (Exodus 15:2). God is great because His work is perfect. He is just, faithful, righteous, and upright (Deuteronomy 32:3). He is to be revered above all gods. No god or goddess comes close in honor (1 Chronicles 16:25, 27). God is in control of the affairs of humankind and reveals secrets (Daniel 2:20–23). God is good, and His love endures forever (Jeremiah 33:11 NLT). God gives us His Spirit as a pledge to salvation (Ephesians 1:14). He brought you to this point in your life through Jesus Christ. Father God knows your sins and weaknesses. God helps you in spite of what's happening (Psalm 34:19). He saves us from all our trouble and fears (Psalm 34:4–6). He gives us spiritual blessings in Christ (Ephesians 1:3). He forgives all our sins and heals us (Psalm 103:3). He is merciful as He blots out our sins and remembers them no more (1 Peter 2:9). Each one of these is a reason to praise God.

The book of Psalms alone is filled with reasons to give praise to our loving, righteous, and holy God. Let's review just a handful of psalms for reasons to recognize God more fully. Each one is full of reasons to praise our God—Psalms 134, 138, 144, 145, 146, 147, 148, 149, and 150.

It is a thrill to know God. As you understand how much there is to God, He begins to reveal a little more of Himself. He does this because you appreciate who He is. He will reveal more profound and hidden things to you.

God really wants us to know His names so that we can know His character better. It's a true honor to discover God more. As you name His titles and positions of authority, you will recognize the many areas of His character. Thus, you can also praise Him for what He does. He is called " I AM", the eternal one, the provider, your healer, the Lord our banner, the Lord who sanctifies, the Lord of peace, the Lord of host, the Lord, my shepherd, the Lord our righteousness, the Lord who is always there, the Way, the truth, the Lord who is life, the Lord who is the light, and the Lord who is the resurrection. God is all of these. You can begin to pray to God with one or more of these names.

You have a bigger and better view of God when you honor Him with your heartfelt praise. One of your purposes in life is to praise God. Praising God leads us to true repentance. You see the real mercy and goodness of God. Praise shall be your lifestyle. This keeps us in our close personal relationship with God.

Because you praise God, He can make a dividing line between you and your enemy. It will keep your enemy from overtaking you. Because you praise God, you are surrounded with shields to ward off the fiery darts of the devil. Because you praise God, you find favor and blessings you don't deserve. Because you praise God, you are free from your past of pain. Salvation is free. Because you praise God, God uses new ways to make you safe and stable with new ideas and financial breaks. Ask Him to put you on solid ground.

Take the time to reflect on the Lord's mighty work of salvation in your life. Isaiah comforted God's people with words that reviewed the many things God does (Isaiah 40 NKJV).

Jeremiah tells Israel to boast about God, "that he understands and knows me, that I am the LORD who exercises kindness, justice and righteousness on earth, for in these I delight" (Jeremiah 9:24 NASB).

Let nothing stop you from praising God.

David gave a heartrendering prayer to praise the Lord in the presence of the whole assembly. He spoke of God's greatness, power, glory, and strengthen. David also named God as ruler of all things. (1 Chronicles 29: 10-13). If you are a thankful person, you are constantly praising Him.

As you praise God, you offer a loving and pleasing sacrifice.

"Praise the LORD. Praise God in his sanctuary; praise him in his mighty heavens. Praise him for his acts of power; praise him for his surpassing greatness … Let everything that has breath praise the LORD. Praise the LORD" (Psalm 150:1–2, 6).

Give More Credit to Others

Since you praise God continually, you see how He works and succeeds through others. Let others know you appreciate what they do. Let us respect and appreciate what others do for us. Give credit to others who serve God's will and do what is right and good. God is working through them. Thank them.

9. Sing Songs to God

"Through Jesus, therefore, let us continually offer to God a sacrifice of praise—the fruit of lips that confess his name" (Hebrews 13:15).

"Let the word of Christ richly dwell within you, with all wisdom, teaching and admonishing one another with psalms and hymns and spiritual songs, singing with thankfulness in your hearts to God" (Colossians 3:16).

"Speaking to one another in psalms and hymns and spiritual songs, singing and making melody with your heart to the Lord" (Ephesians 5:19).

"I will praise You, O LORD, with my whole heart; I will tell of your marvelous works, I will be glad and rejoice in You; I will sing praise to Your name, O Most High" (Psalm 9:1–2 NKJV).

"For what you have done I will always praise you in the presence of your faithful people. And I will hope in your name, for your name is good" (Psalm 52:9).

Singing is so important to God that He had families dedicated to singing praises as part of certain special ceremonies and daily worship. David told the leaders of the Levites to appoint their brothers and sisters as singers who could sing joyful songs. In addition, they would play musical instruments to go along with their singing. Kenaniah, the head Levite, was in charge of the singing. It was his responsibility because he was so skillful at singing (1 Chronicles 15:16, 27 NLT). Some directed the singers. There were male and female singers. In addition, certain Levite families dedicated their lives to playing musical instruments for the singers in service to God.

During service the first family of Levite singers sang about how great God was. When the ark was moved to Jerusalem, the singers said, "He indeed is good for His loving kindness is everlasting" (1 Chronicles 5:13 NASB). When Jehoshaphat went out to defeat the Moab and Ammon, he appointed men to sing to the Lord and to praise Him for the splendor of His holiness. They said, "Give thanks to the LORD, for his love endures forever" (2 Chronicles 20:21 NASB). When the wall was rebuilt, the gatekeepers and singers were appointed to serve the house of God (Nehemiah 12: 27 NLT). When the wall of Jerusalem was completed, two large choirs gave thanks (Nehemiah 12: 31). Musicians were among the divisions of the Levites assigned to sing and play praises to God. (1 Chronicles 25: 1, 6-8). Whenever something important was happening , singers and musicians were involved in the services.

So the tradition of singing songs to God is well documented. Music was and still is a central part of worship. God loves this as David, Solomon, and Nehemiah understood. This is a very natural way to praise and thank God. The countless deeds God has done, is doing, and will do should fill our mouths with joy. Likewise, there are endless reasons to sing to God. He wants us to glorify and honor Him with our mouths and our actions.

God has blessed certain families, relatives, and individuals with singing abilities. You can hear the songs and see the dedication of time and strength they put into serving God in this way. It is truly a joy to hear inspired singing. They are using their singing as a ministry for God.

There are hundreds of great singers in the world. You can hear and see the love and gratitude they have for God. This is pure joy.

Praising and thanking God is a great expression of heartfelt emotion. One way you can talk to God is through music. Words from scripture or songs from the heart can give you a chance to tell God that you appreciate all He is and everything He does. We get the chance to review the person, work, and glory of Christ. God has given us songs to sing from scripture.

We all can sing to God in our own way. Many families and individuals are blessed with an outstanding ability to sing and grace us with heartfelt sharing. God is so pleased. We can sing in a choir. We can all sing as part of the congregation. We all can make a joyful noise to God. When people dedicate their singing talent to praising and thanking God, we all benefit a lot. Singing to God enhances the worship service and our refocus on the one true God. It is pure joy to sing to God. You can see and hear the Holy Spirit inspiring us to share those feelings and truths. Sing to God while at home. Sing to God while you drive. Do your very best when you sing to God. We can all have a musical ministry for God.

Singing songs and playing instruments is only one of the ways we worship our great and awesome God. How well and how often we sing is not the measuring stick for outstanding worship services. Rather it is how well we keep Jesus at the center of our lives. The Holy Spirit points us to Jesus. He inspires us not only to sing songs to praise and thank Jesus but to live lives that express praise and thanks to Jesus. This is what truly glorifies God.

There are several genres that praise and thank God in song. There are hundreds of songs in each of those genres. Some types include gospel music, Christian rap, country western gospel, Christian classical/sacred, contemporary worship, Christian metal, and Christian pop. There are thousands of outstanding heartfelt songs to pick from. God loves variety. You can find some of these songs on YouTube and other music sites. What you say to God makes a difference. God enjoys all these songs.

Several Old Testament leaders sang songs to praise our God. Moses recited the words of his song before the whole congregation of Israel (Deuteronomy 32:1–43 NJKV). David sang a song of praise to God (2 Samuel 22:1–51 NKJV). Isaiah also sang a song of praise to God (Isaiah 12 NKJV).

We should want to sing praise from the heart since God does so much. He forgives all your sins, redeems your life, heals your diseases, gives you mercy instead of judgment, keeps every promise He makes, makes financial breakthroughs, serves as a source of spiritual truths, bring you closer to Him, delivers your from sin, saves you from all fears, leads you to repentance, forgives you, shows mercy in spite of my sins, and changes you for the better. We are sanctified in Him and justified in Him. He protects you, keeps you from your enemy, frees you from your past, and helps us become new creatures in Christ. These are all great reasons to sing to God.

As you sing the many and mighty songs to God, you again offer a sacrifice. He is very pleased.

Raise your voice to sing in joy and glorify our awesome God. William McDowell has two great songs about giving yourself to God as a living sacrifice—"I Give Myself Away" and "Withholding Nothing."

Go to appendix 2 for a short list of songs to God.

10. Be Thankful to God and Others

Thanksgiving Offering

"But giving thanks is a sacrifice that truly honors me. If you keep to my path, I will reveal to you the salvation of God" (Psalm 50:23 NLT).

"Through Him then, let us continually offer up a sacrifice of praise to God, that is, the fruit of lips that give thanks to His name" (Hebrews 13:15 NASB).

"Let the word of Christ richly dwell within you, with all wisdom teaching and admonishing one another with psalms and hymns and spiritual songs, singing with thankfulness in your hearts to God. Whatever you do in word or deed, do all in the name of the Lord Jesus, giving thanks through Him to God the Father" (Colossians 3:16–17 NASB).

"Shout with joy to the LORD, all the earth! Worship the LORD with gladness. Come before him, singing with joy. Acknowledge that the LORD is God! He made us, and we are his. We are his people, the sheep of his pasture. Enter his gates with thanksgiving; go into his courts with praise. Give thanks to him and praise his name. For the LORD is good.

His unfailing love continues forever, and his faithfulness continues to each generation" (Psalm 100 NLT).

"So thank God for his marvelous love, for his miracle mercy to the children he loves; Offer thanksgiving sacrifices, tell the world what he's done—sing it out!" (Psalm 107:22 The Message).

Giving thanks to God is a way of offering a sacrifice of thanksgiving. The sacrifices of thanksgiving we offer today are not animals on an altar but "the fruit of lips that give thanks to His name," "singing with thanksgiving in [our] hearts to God," grateful attitudes and actions, and "acceptable service with reverence and awe" toward God. God gave Israel the offering of thanksgiving so it would acknowledge He was the one true God and the source of everything they had. God wants us to do the same today.

Always go before God in the attitude of being thankful. Then He knows you appreciate Him. He knows you recognize He can do the impossible. He knows you understand His love is unconditional.

It's very good to give God thanks. Singing with thankfulness in our hearts to God shows that we have a grateful attitude. This is an acceptable service to God with respect and awe. This pleases Him (Hebrews 12:28–29).

Certain people were appointed to the role of offering praise and thanks to God through singing and playing instruments (1 Chronicles 16: 4, 41). We do the same thing today. That's how important it is to God. Singers and choirs also are appointed to make petitions, to give thanks, and to praise the Lord, and Father God through songs.

We are to bring a thanksgiving offering before we do anything. When Judah went into battle against its enemy, singers offering thanks became a source of confidence (2 Chronicles 20:21 NASB). They went before the army and began singing, "Give thanks to the LORD for His lovingkindness is everlasting."

God made His move to give them victory. It showed that God was fighting for them. Likewise, we should thank God for His involvement in our battles against our enemies. He will give us victory. Start your day by praising and thanking God. Start your prayer by praising God with thanksgiving (Matthew 6:9) Remember how great, loving, and powerful our living God truly is. King David praised the Lord in the presence of the whole assembly. He began by saying, "Praise be to you, LORD, the God of our father Israel. Now, our God, we give you thanks, and praise your glorious name." (1 Chronicles 29: 10, 13).

Always thank God no matter what circumstances you find yourself in. While you are in the problem, thank God for the answer and solution that's best for you. He will always do what is best and just. That attitude of thanks helps you get through any problem quicker. You know things are going to improve and all work out. You just have to endure through situations.

Being thankful is the key to releasing the supernatural power of God in your life. He gives you grace, peace, humility, faith, and salvation. These help you serve Him with excitement. Miracles come from the spirit of thanks.[20]

You are not in the will of God when you don't give thanks. When you complain, you find fault in the genius and power of God. When you complain, you deny His greatness. You are told to thank God for His many deeds because He really cares for you.

We are to thank God for so much! We thank Him for His wonderful acts toward the children of humankind. He is a source of strength. He gives fair judgments. He keeps His promises. He gives us goodness, unfailing love, light, loving-kindness, salvation, and mercy. He provides for us. He is our deliverer in battles. He answers prayers, and He is compassionate. He is our source of refuge and unity among the believers. He is above all gods, a perfect creation, a source of truth. He is omnipresence and omniscience, and He hates evil and wickedness. He protects us, sanctifies and redeems us, and forgives us our sins. He is our stronghold and deliverer, righteous in all His deeds, executing justice for the oppressed. These are some of the

---

[20] Charles Stanley Pastor, "Be Thankful," From *Pastors Heart Letter*, November 2017.

reasons we should thank God. These are also great reasons for singing to God. The book of Psalms is full of reasons we honor and give glory to God.

You should keep thanking our God. Always give thanks to God for everything He does. We, along with the twenty-four elders, four living creatures, and thousands of angels will spend our eternal existence always praising and thanking God (Revelation 4:8–11; 5:11–12). We will finally see what He has done, what He is doing, and what He will do for everlasting time. They see His power, person, and grace. They have been praising and thanking God since the beginning of creation billions of years ago.

God has great plans for your eternal growth and development. This is love on a whole other level.

Stay in the habit of thanking God for wonderful deeds because His character is perfect, holy, and righteous. He loves beyond what we can understand right now. Give thanks to God as a habit. When you wake up, thank and praise God. Begin with what God has already done. Remember His works, goodness, spiritual gifts, family health, freedoms, grace, spiritual knowledge, and salvation.[21]

Always be grateful and thankful! He deserves it! He expects it too. Jesus healed ten men with leprosy. Only one returned to Jesus to praise and thank Him. Jesus asked, "Were not all ten cleansed? Where are the other nine?" (Luke 17:12--19).

Your truthful thanks to God glorifies Him. This tells God you really appreciate what He does for you. Be grateful for His deep love for you.

"And whatever you do, whether in word or deed, do it all in the name of the Lord Jesus, giving thanks to God the Father through Him" (Colossians 3:15, 17).

---

[21] Mike Booze Pastor, "The Breakfast of Champions: Habit of Thanksgiving," Faith Community in Shreveport, LA, November 2016.

Being a thankful person shows God that you appreciate who He is to you and to the world.

Appreciate Others

Since God wants us to be thankful for the countless ways He helps us, He also want us to appreciate our neighbor. God touches the hearts of many people in your life so that they are kind to you. They desire to do what's just, right, and good. Thank others for the little, as well as big, acts of kindness toward you. They enacted these mostly from the heart. Sometimes they will do what's right out of duty or simply because they feel responsible. That's why an unknown person can walk up to you and give you some much-needed money, encouragement, or kindness. That's why a difficult situation is made possible because a person has been inspired to do something for you (e.g., buying a certain item you need, hiring you, starting a certain business because of you, making just the right contact, etc.). God has told them to do certain things for you. They are obeying God. Be aware that God inspired them. Be grateful and thankful to others who show you what God has in mind for you.

11. Keep Your Peace, Joy, and Hope

Jesus is our source of peace, joy, and hope. Let's discuss peace first.

"Don't worry about anything; instead, pray about everything. Tell God what you need, and thank him for all he has done. Then you will experience God's peace, which exceeds anything we can understand. His peace will guard your hearts and minds as you live in Christ ... Keep putting into practice all you have learned and received from me—everything you heard from me and saw me doing. Then the God of peace will be with you" (Philippians 4:6–7, 9 NLT).

There are several areas of peace. One is inner peace, which is what Jesus promised. Second, there is peace with God through your faith in Jesus. Third, there's the interpersonal peace that exist in our relationships with others (Romans 12:18 NASB). I will focus mainly on our close relationship with Jesus and how it affects us.

When we receive Christ as our Savior, a spirit of tranquility and freedom enters our lives. The peace of Christ is found through making Him more important than anything or anyone in your life. Keep your mind on God.

Peace is from the Father and Jesus Christ, and it comes through the Holy Spirit (John 16:33). When the Spirit is poured out on us from heaven, the work of righteousness will began. It will also bring quietness and confidence forever. You will be at rest.

The Lord is our peace. Recall the time when the disciples were out on a boat and a fierce storm came upon them. The boat was beginning to fill with water. Jesus was asleep. They woke Jesus up and pleaded for His help. He quickly calmed the storm. Jesus is able to keep us calm during physical difficulties like fires, storms, hurricanes, floods, and earthquakes. He also is able to be there during spiritual situations. The devil seeks to deceive you about the truth concerning God and your wonderful relationship with Him.

There is a way that leads to perfect peace (Isaiah 26:3–4 NLT). Remain faithful to God. Keep your mind fixed on Him (Romans 14:19 NJKV). Since you trust in the Lord, you will have peace.

This is done as we become filled with the Spirit (Galatians 5:22–23 The Message). As you do what you are supposed to do, peace is in you—abiding in the Lord (John 14:27 NJKV), seeking Him in prayer, trusting Him, turning away from evil, doing good (Psalm 34:14), loving the commands of God (Psalm 119:165), speaking the truth (Zechariah 8:16), allowing the Spirit to control your mind (Romans 8:6 NLT), and doing what you have been taught. These acts of love are works of peace. This is how we conform to Jesus.

God wants us to have peace. The kingdom of God is a matter of righteousness, peace, and joy. Anyone who serves Christ in this way is pleasing to God. God wants us to follow the things that make for peace. God wants us to edify one another, not offend others with bad examples. Don't condemn yourself by what you allow yourself to do, and instead do right things in faith (Romans 14:17, 19–23).

God called us to peace. We know God causes all things to work together for the good to those who love Him. We are justified and soon will be glorified with Jesus Christ (Romans 8:28–31). Jesus's death and resurrection gives us a sense of confidence. We know Jesus gave us victory over sin, death, and the devil. We know the gift of grace sets us free.

The blessed life is not out of reach. Regardless of what is going on around us, regardless of the violence on every street corner, regardless of global apathy, our God reigns! He is still in control, and everything is going to be all right. When we walk with Jesus Christ into the battle, we are already victorious. The blessed life can be ours because we are children of the Most High!

Even though a war wages with the *powers* and *principalities* of darkness, there is no need to fear. The real battle belongs to the Lord. No weapon that is formed against you shall prosper. As a servant of the Lord, you have been promised peace, righteousness, security, and triumph over all opposition. No matter what is happening, keep your prayer life strong, and stay focused on Jesus.

Peace will stay with you despite unexpected events and surprises. You may experience illness, the sudden death of a loved one, or a loss of a job. When you ask God for help, you are reminded that Christ is always with you. We can ask God to be with our family members from anywhere in the world.

I enjoyed talking and being with my twin sister. She suffered from diabetes and its complications. Both she and husband had health difficulties before they died, but both also had peace in Jesus. How they lived and what they said always made a deep impression on me. They said, "Look at what my God has done for me. Everything happens for a reason. God has done too much for me to get angry with Him. Just believe and have faith in Him. He knows how much I can bear." You will have a high level of confidence and faith in God.

God wants us to really enjoy His peace. When you trust Him, His peace flows in your heart. You will have a positive and relaxing attitude. It comforts you (2 Corinthians 1:3–6 NLT). We enjoy health and healing (Jeremiah 33:6 NJKV). We are free of guilt and worry since we rest our cause in God's hands. We are content with whatever state we are in (Philippians 4:11–12). There is a sense of certainty and security. We are bold and confident that God will keep His promises. We are also very thankful that we have the privilege of walking with Christ. This true happiness is found in your heart as you seek peace with others. You are a peacemaker. You are living the gospel of peace. You have joy and peace in believing the scriptures.

You realize the Lord is steadily building a godly character in you. You are sealed and secured as His child. You are being empowered to obey and serve Him. This gives us deeper faith and peace that God is working for us, with us, and in us.

Life with Jesus is full. There is joy, peace, and happiness since you trust and identify with Him.

"Let the peace of Christ rule in your heart, since as members of one body you were called to peace. And be thankful" (Colossians 3:15).

Keep Your Joy in God

The second area of strength and health is joy.

"Let them give thanks to the LORD for his unfailing love and his wonderful deeds for men. Let them sacrifice thank offering and tell of his works with songs of joy" (Psalm 107:21–22).

"O send out Your light truth, let them lead me; Then I will go to the altar of God, To God my exceeding joy; And upon the lyre I shall praise You, O God, my God" (Psalm 43:3–4).

"For You make him most blessed forever; You make him joyful with gladness in your presence" (Psalm 21:6 NASB).

God Himself is full of joy. He has kept His youth and zest for life. He is joyful all the time. He is full of love, happiness, and celebration. He is enthusiastic and compassionate about what He does.

We get that rejoicing spirit from God. He is very excited about the plan of salvation, which is moving on schedule—the birth of Christ, the death of Christ, the resurrection of Jesus Christ, the Holy Spirit descending on His church, and the return of Jesus.

He and the angels rejoice when a new believer is baptized into His family. That's why we give a handshake of fellowship to those baptized members. He rejoices when one lost sheep is found and brought back to His flock.

God is preparing a place of responsibility. We are meant to be in His presence, forever glorifying Him and growing. We will serve Jesus Christ.

You are also full of joy because of the things you do. You obey God. Your life is surrendered to His Word as you follow the Word. You give the glory to God. If you are doing these things, it's because of the mercy and love of God. You do these things because you know God is so forgiving. You realize God's grace makes a difference.

After you are forgiven by God, you become joyful. God doesn't stay mad with you (Psalm 30:5 NJKV). When you see God has accepted your sacrifices (of sin, of devoting all to Him, and of seeking to fellowship with Him), you will shout for joy and worship gladly (Leviticus 9:22–24).

As we think and focus on helping others, you improve your relationships with them. Giving and sharing becomes a better way of life for you. This is what Jesus does. You should joyfully help a person in need. Don't even expect a thank-you. Joy will overflow in your spirit.

God is excited and compassionate about you. He loves the way His children respond to the way He is guiding and leading. He is delighted, and He is so happy about our success.

He does not want you to be worried or anxious about anything. Joy comes during and after you go through a problem trusting God. He comforts us in all our troubles so that you can comfort others. When we walk with Jesus, every day can be a great day. This is true no matter the circumstances.

He wants you to have a full and enjoyable life every day (John 10:10 AMPC). Celebrate today in spite of problems. You know God is with you even in your periods of depression, loneliness, addiction, anger, or heartache. Just keep looking to Jesus. Keep leaning on Him for strength. Keep your joy!

The only person who can make you happy is your Savior, the Lord Jesus Christ.

As you can see, peace, joy, and hope are closely related. Being at peace with Jesus brings us joy and strengthens our hope for eternal life.

Know that God is for you. God is with you. God is in you through the Holy Spirit. We have so much to look forward to. God Himself keeps us secure. Since we have an awesome future ahead us and outstanding resources available to us, we have every reason to be full of joy! We are going to succeed! You are a child of God! Keep your joy flowing.

Our prayers should be full of praise and thanksgiving to God. As a result, we are to be full of joy.

Keep your joy. Let others see your joy. Praise God for His desire to fill your life with joy.

"If you obey my commands, you will remain in my love, just as I obeyed my Father's command and remain in his love. I have told you this so that my joy may be in you and that your joy may be complete" (John 15:10–12).

"May the God of hope fill you with all joy and peace as you trust in him. So that you may overflow with hope by the power of the Holy Spirit" (Romans 15:13).

Keep your Hope in God

"I pray that God, the source of hope, will fill you completely with joy and peace because you can trust in him. Then you will overflow with confident hope through the power of the Holy Spirit" (Romans 15:13 NLT).

"All praise to God, the Father of our Lord Jesus Christ. It is by his great mercy that we have been born again, because God raised Jesus Christ from the dead. Now we live with great expectation, and we have a priceless inheritance—an inheritance that is kept in heaven for you, pure and undefiled, beyond the reach of change and decay. And through your faith, God is protecting you by his power until you receive this salvation, which is ready to be revealed on the last day for all to see" (1 Peter 1:3–5 NLT).

Hope is something you desire and wish for in the future. Our hope of success and eternal life only comes from God.

Father God gives us hope because He lives by hope Himself. Our God set before Himself a hope so great that He will not be able to realize it. The goal that He strives for is so vast and eternally involved that He will never achieve it. This is God's eternal plan. The universe will continually be expanded and/or be recreated. Thus more galaxies and more planets. Thus more places to develop human life to become children of God. Thus more challenges to create new animals and plants similar to earth but different.

God proposes to bring you into His family to share His divine nature completely. He plans to bring us into glory like Jesus. He wants us to be holy. He wants us to have His character and to be full of love, peace, and joy like Him.

We have an eternal reason to live. God has a practical plan. He has said that He never wants an end to the expansion of His heavenly kingdom. His plan is to continue adding sons and daughters who look, feel, and act with same self-generating eternal spirit as He has forever! God has a hope that not even He can ever fulfill—endless, eternal, forever creating an ever-expanding family to enjoy and rule the great creation He has already made. God has a practical, interesting, challenging, and ongoing plan that gives all an eternal reason for living. We will have an eternal job of creating, governing, and further developing humankind. Our Father gave us eternal encouragement and good hope (2 Thessalonians 2:16, 17). There is a glorious future with God. Cherish this greatest hope God offers to you.

Our hope is centered around the resurrection of Jesus Christ. He is now gloried. Everything is now possible through His victory over sin and death. He is working to make everyone fellow heirs of the kingdom.

The Bible is the basis for our hope. As you read and study the Word, you realize Jesus is everywhere in the scriptures (Psalm 78:1–7 NLT). The next generation will know the glorious deeds of Jesus Christ. They will learn about His power and His mighty wonders. They will obey the commands of God. We will only gain the inheritance of God because the Holy Spirit guides and leads us.

Hope in God comes through our faith that God keeps His Word (Romans 4:18, 21 NLT). He keeps every promise. Abraham's growing faith in the promises of God brought glory to God.

When you speak God's powerful Word over your life, then real and lasting changes will happen. You are positive in how you think, talk, and live. Use your words to proclaim the hope, blessings, faith, and encouragement you have because Jesus is in your life. Be a source of hope to others.

Trust God to get you through all your difficulties. There is a power you can plug into that will help you handle the things you can't handle on your own. You are never alone. That's good news.

Once you see the great hope before you, you will praise God continually.

You grow in your level of hope by enduring and achieving victory in trails. You know God is right beside you (Romans 5:1–5). You build longer patience, and your experiences deepen as you look to God.

Show your high hope as you interact and talk to others. You will talk about God. Others will see that you depend on God to bring you through hard situations and issues. Others will see that you have a deep and loving relationship with God. You can never stop giving God the credit for the outcomes of your decisions. You will praise and thank God for all He does in your life.

Our hope for eternal life with God is secure (Job 11:18). The believer already possesses this hope. We are fully assured that an inheritance beyond our wildest imagination awaits us.

Fix your hope completely on the grace given to you because of Jesus Christ (1 Peter 1:13). Hold on to your confidence in Jesus and your service to Him for all eternity. Your prayers will be full of praise toward God because you deeply love Him. As you trust in God's holy name, you will be filled with peace and joy. With God, there is living hope.

Therefore, whatever difficulties you have, endure them to the end. They won't compare to your glorious future with God. This is our great hope. This hope drives us to grow and change so that we become more like Jesus Christ.

"But blessed are those who trust in the LORD and made the LORD their hope and confidence" (Jeremiah 17:7 NLT)

PART FOUR – THE FAT

Strength and Health in Finding and Doing God's Purpose

The fat illustrates general health, energy, and strength. This shows the use of our strength and health to glorify God. Use God's strength to get many jobs done when you are weak. This also shows a blessing of good health and abundance. God wants you to enjoy your life right now. He wants you to live a full overflowing abundant life.

When God tells you to do something, do it. Since God knows what He is doing all the time, follow His lead or suggestion. He uses people to bless or help others. Realize that everything God does is right and just.

Today's saints desire to love God with all of their heart, soul, mind, and strength, and to love their neighbor as themselves. This means totally surrendering and devoting themselves to God.

The washing of the legs and inwards was done before the animal was burned up on an altar. Today Christians need to be spiritually pure not only in what they do, but also in their desires. Jesus will make his church holy by the water through the Word, the Holy Spirit (Ephesians 5:26). God will test our work to see if it stands. God's word is a fire. These fiery trials test our readiness to be the bride of Christ. Your character and faith must be proven. You will be tested and tried. The Holy Spirit will help us through those trials and temptations. The Holy Spirit will convict you in regard to sin, righteousness, and judgement (John 16:7-9,13-15 NKJV). He will guide us into all truth. This cleansing will help us go on to a complete and mature way of life. The Holy Spirit helps, guides, and leads us. Learn to listen to Him.

Our salvation is not dependent on the burnt offering. After we are reconciled to God by confessing our sins and are accepted by Him (sin offering, trespass offering), We want to voluntarily offer our lives to God. We now want to renew and restore our relationship. God wants an even closer walk with you. He always does.

12. Seek and Do the Will of God

"You take no delight in sacrifices or offerings. Now that you have made me listen, I finally understand—you don't require burnt offerings or sin offerings. Then I said, 'Look, I have come. As it is written about me in the Scriptures: I take joy in doing your will, my God, for your instructions are written on my heart'" (Psalm 40:6–8 NLT).

"Jesus said to them, My food is to do the will of Him who sent Me and to accomplish His work" (John 4:34 NASB).

"I have come down from heaven, not to do My will, but the will of Him who sent me" (John 6:38 NASB).

Jesus sought to do the will of the Father. The main purpose for His coming to live a human life was to give up His life as a sin offering for humankind. He took the place of the wicked. He lived a perfect life to satisfy Father God's requirements. Then He conquered sin and death. Now humanity is sanctified, and the wall that separates us from the holy God is removed when we repent of sin.

God wants us to understand His will or purpose (Ephesians 5:15–17; Colossians 1:9–14). He will teach us His will (Psalm 143:10). He wants us to be filled with the knowledge of His will. We must learn to listen to what He tells us to do.

The Holy Spirit will give us wisdom and understanding to really do the will of God. The Holy Spirit knows the will of God. He even gives you the talents, abilities, and desire to accomplish His will. Find out what you have that you can bring to bear to do God's will (Colossians 1:9–14). Use those resources under the influence of Holy Spirit as you are in service to God.

Someone said, "Life's greatest discovery is to know the will of God ... and life's greatest satisfaction is to do the will of God." When you know His will for your life and do His will, your life is filled with purpose. This brings unbelievable joy, peace, and satisfaction.

When you know your purpose, you are at peace. You are content with whatever circumstances you are in. You know everything is going to work out.

You have a choice. If you decide to reject God's will for your life, you will miss out on the best God has planned for you. If you choose to do God's will, you will fulfill God's real purpose of eternal life for you. You will also enjoy life and feel goal-oriented. You'll be excited about doing whatever God designs for you.

God has the ultimate level of expectation and purpose for His Kingdom, Jesus Christ, and His children. There are four overall areas that cover everything He is doing.

First, God is "advancing His kingdom" to rule over the entire creation. God can provide what you need. There is no scarcity with God (Matthew 6:33). In due time, His kingdom will be fully recognized by all. His kingdom will cover the whole earth. Nations will go to Jerusalem to recognize the new way.

Second, it is God's will that you have eternal life with Him forever (John 6:38–40).

Third, God is honoring Jesus Christ as our Lord with power and authority. Are you surrendering all to Jesus? He is our just judge. He is our Lord and Savior. He is King of Kings and Lord of Lords. He is the only way to the Father and salvation. It is the Father's good pleasure to bring everything together under the authority of Christ—everything in heaven and on earth (Ephesians 9:10).

Finally, God wants to be glorified in all we do. He makes everything work out. He wants humankind to recognize and acknowledge how great He is really. We need to realize the world exists for the glory of God's grace revealed in the saving work of Jesus. He wants His children to point back to Him as the reason for their success, peace, joy, and hope. You should desire to really know Him. You should thank Him for guiding and leading you to such amazing actions. Keep pointing out that God deserves the credit for any good you do. Keep pointing out that He deserves the glory and honor. As we live lives that cause people to praise God, you glorify God. He wants to keep doing a lot through you.

Jesus doesn't want any part of your life wasted. He can even use your suffering for some good. By overcoming your suffering, you can point others to Jesus. So trust Him. He can turn your failure into a great success. He can turn your situation into a testimony. Your sin, your bad decision, your following temptation, your selfish behavior can be a lesson. Share with the unknowing, what you learned. Warn them of your mistake. Are you patient with God like He has been patient with you? He knows when and how to let you know what He has in mind for you.

As you renew your mind through the Holy Spirit, you'll be able to test and prove what is His good, pleasing, and perfect will (Romans 12:2 NKJV).

God works in you so that you act according to His good purpose (Philippians 3:13 NLT).

When God does reveal to you what He wants you to do, start right away. Most of the time, He has already prepared you for the assignment without you knowing it. You have the skills, abilities, interest, and experience. God is now telling you to focus them so that you can do a certain thing at a certain time in a certain way. Remember Abraham, Noah, Moses, Esther, Joseph, Jeremiah, Daniel, David, Ananias, Paul, and the countless men and women of faith. You, too, have a purpose that God desires for you to fulfill.

The assignment He starts with you may be very small. You may just give an encouraging word to a person, or you may give an unknown person a certain amount of money and say, "God told me to do this." He may inspire you to donate your clothes to help a friend or a stranger. He sees you obey in the small matters. He is preparing you for some big things.

The mission may be very involved. He may want you to sing, organize, write, cook, manage, build, explain the gospel, train, teach, write songs, play a sport, start a business, work as a craftsman, graduate from college with a certain major, work for a certain company, start your own company, and so forth. God wants you to use your talents and abilities to serve others and thus glorify Him. Of course, God knows what is right for you at a certain time in your life. Trust Him. He knows what He is doing. Finish each assignment God gives you, or keep working on it.

When you are where you supposed to be and doing what you supposed to be doing, everything works out. Things just seem to get better. Here are two examples. A church friend of mine is a self-employed master welder. At first, he was worried about striking out on his own. Then God connected him with his first customers. His business took off. He has been welding for several years now. Today he gets two to three calls a day about jobs. He is busy busy. He is close to God and is friendly. Another guy received a great suggestion from a friend of his about where to locate his barbecue business. He already was a great cook. The person suggested he place his pits along the well-traveled street that led to the only large grocery store in the small town. He tried it on a Friday, and he had a large number of customers. They asked if he could come back on Saturday. Now he has a building with a window counter, three pits that are enclosed, and a cold storage building. His wife and relatives all pitched in to help. He went from only being open on Friday and Saturday to adding Thursday. Now people can't wait for him to open. He also uses his barbecue business to cater events. They received four orders in two weeks for fifty rib eyes at each event. He is a friendly Christian who makes people feel at ease. God will make sure you are a success, but you must keep praising and thanking God. That's what they both do.

When you know your purpose, you are at peace. You will have the courage to move forward. God will open doors for you at the right time. Recognize this and walk through the door. Then praise and thank God.

You are very unique. You will see something special about God that only you will recognize and fulfill. You have been blessed with a unique set of spiritual gifts (1 Corinthians 12:4–11), a unique personality, and unique life experience. God desires to use them in unique ways.

Understand God isn't finished with you. Your best days are ahead of you. God has a purpose for your life! As a believer, you are encouraged to keep growing and guiding others to Jesus. You realize you are important to God. You know God loves you.

Don't get tired of doing His will. Ask God to keep using you. Ask God to give you more understanding and direction. He is leading you to do great things. You are in the most secure place as you accomplish His will.

There is a common purpose for all followers of Christ. They should

- be sanctified, avoid sexual immorality, control their own bodies in a honorable way, not wrong or take advantage of their brothers or sisters in Christ (1 Thessalonians 4:3–5);
- live holy lives (1 Thessalonians 4:7);
- be joyful always, pray always, give thanks in all circumstances (1 Thessalonians 5:16–18);
- be witnesses (Acts 1:8);
- be humble always (James 4:6);
- be conformed to the image of Jesus Christ (Romans 8:29); and
- have eternal life with Him forever (John 6:40).

As we mature, we will be more like Christ in character and actions. You will show the fruits of the Spirit. A mature Christian will seek God's will in everything. This is the underlying question: Is this God's will, and is it keeping me close to God?

As we do the will of God, He will make His abode with us, dwell with us, and manifest Himself to us more and more. Your confidence will keep growing.

The real question is this: What is the purpose of your life? God created you to not only live for eternity with Him but to be like Him. You will always be learning and growing. Realize you are important to God. Therefore, confess your sins to God. Accept Jesus' sacrifice of His blood. He has plans and purposes for you. You will be tested. So trust God to bring you through anything. Live to do His will, and follow Jesus Christ's example. Love Him and your fellow man. Share the gospel with those who give you the opportunity. Give glory to God from the heart. Dr. Charles Stanley answered the question of our purpose of life very well.

God looks forward to being in your life and being a vital part of your identity in the Holy Spirit. He looks forward to sharing His plans for you directly. He looks forward to doing His will through you more and more.

Doing the will of God is another act of worshipping and offering yourself to Him.

"Whoever does the will of my Father in heaven is my brother and sister and mother" (Matthew 12:50).

Living for God is doing God's will. "As a result, they do not live the rest of their earthly lives for evil human desires, but rather for the will of God" (1 Peter 4:2).

13. Delight in the Mercy of God

Show Mercy to Others

"I desire mercy and not sacrifice, and the knowledge of God more than burnt offerings" (Hosea 6:6 NKJV).

"He has shown you, O man, what is good; And what does the Lord require of you But to do justly, To love mercy, And to walk humbly with your God?" (Micah 6:8 NKJV).

"For if you forgive other people when they sin against you, your heavenly Father will also forgive you" (Matthew 6:14)

We all want someone to show mercy to us when we mess up, make wrong decisions, or simply do the wrong thing. We are ready to ask for forgiveness.

Being merciful is showing compassion. It's having a willingness to spare, not always demanding immediate justice. You are willing to help, and you are ready to place yourself in someone else shoes.

We certainly want God to give us mercy. We know we must have His mercy. Otherwise, we won't make it. We sin every day. So we need mercy from God every day.

God is very merciful. He is compassionate and gracious, slow to anger, abounding in love. God describes Himself to Moses as He gets ready to give the commandments. God said, "The Lord, the Lord, the compassionate and gracious God, slow to anger, abounding in love and faithfulness, maintaining love to thousands, and forgiving wickedness, rebellion and sin. Yet he does not leave the guilty unpunished" (Exodus 34:6–7a). God delights in showing mercy. He is very rich in mercy. He shows that mercy to whomever He pleases. This is His nature.

The best way to get mercy and forgiveness is to admit you did wrong. Openly tell the person you wronged about what you did. Then ask for mercy. Reveal that you will not do that again. Otherwise, when the wronged person finds out what you did, he or she will only have a very short supply of mercy. "People who conceal their sins will not prosper, but if they confess and turn away from them, they will receive mercy" (Proverbs 28:13 NLT).

God wants you to show mercy to others and forgive them as well. "Blessed are the merciful, for they will be shown mercy" (Matthew 5:7). Everything will work for you.

However, if you refuse to act kindly and merciful to others, you can hardly expect to be treated with mercy. Kind mercy is better than harsh judgment every time. Jesus tells a story about a master who forgave a slave for a massive debt. He could have jailed him, his wife, and his children to paid it off. The slave asked for forgiveness. The lord of that slave felt compassion and forgave him of the debt.

But the same forgiven slave told a fellow slave, "Pay back what you owe." This lowly slave also pleaded for patience. But the forgiven slave "was unwilling and went and threw him in prison until he should pay back what was owed." So then his fellow slaves told their lord all that had happened. That lord summoned the forgiven slave. He called that forgiven slave wicked. The lord got very angry and put this first slave in jail to pay all that was owed to him. Jesus concluded by saying, "My heavenly Father will do the same to you, if each of you does not forgive his brother from your heart" (Matthew 18:23–35).

"There will be no mercy for those who have not shown mercy to others. But if they have been merciful, God will be merciful when he judges you" (James 2:13 NLT).

Since we know God is merciful and forgiving, don't hesitate to ask God for mercy. He is ready and willing to do that. Likewise, don't hesitate to forgive others who ask or don't ask.

Actually, when you forgive others, you are set free from that debt. Fellowship with the person can be restored. The only debt we should have is one of loving our fellow men and women. Also, forgiving helps us rely more fully on the Lord. We know God is the one who makes it possible. Remember God meets all our needs, including fairness and justice. We forgive because we have Christ. We know Christ would forgive, and He expects us to forgive as well. So let go of the hurt and anger you have toward the person who wronged you. As a result of forgiving others, you become useful to God again. When you refuse to forgive others, you are laid aside. God won't exult someone whose life contradicts what He wants others to see in Himself—love and forgiveness. You become ineffective. Forgiving restores our usefulness to God. We also recover our fellowship level with the Father. Now we are pleasing to God. We benefit from forgiving others as much as the people we are forgiving.

Delight in knowing how loving and compassionate our God is when we confess our sins. He loves us as we are. He is patient with us. Jesus never turned down a request. Just call out, "Lord, have mercy on me."

"Where is a god who can compare with you—wiping the slate clean of guilt, turning a blind eye, a deaf ear, to the past sins of your purged and precious people? You don't nurse your anger and don't stay angry long, for mercy is your specialty. That's what you love most. And compassion is on its way to us. You'll stamp out our wrongdoing. You'll sink our sins to the bottom of the ocean" (Micah 7:18–19 The Message).

It's in your ability to show mercy to those who need forgiveness. It is also good for you and your well-being. You are happy when you resist hurt feelings, competition, jealously, envy, and judging others. When you show that mercy, you know God is pleased. You know God is with you. Always remember to show others mercy (Ephesians 4:32). He sees you offer mercy and forgiveness to others as He shows mercy to you. This is good.

14. Trust God Completely

"Offer the righteous sacrifices and trust in the Lord" (Psalm 4:5 NASB).

"Trust in Him at all times, O people; Pour out your heart before Him; God is a refuge for us" (Psalm 62:8).

"Blessed is the man who believes and trusts in and relies on the Lord and whose hope and confidence is the Lord" (Jeremiah 17:7 AMPC).

We were created for a close relationship of faith and trust with our Lord. This is the essence of our close relationship with God. He should be able to trust you to do what's right.

There are ways to show your trust in God.

- Don't lean on your own understanding.
- Put your faith in Jesus.
- Ask and know He will deliver you from all troubles (Psalm 34:6, 19).
- Expect answers to your prayers.
- Don't worry about anything.

- Don't be afraid (Psalm 56:3, 10–11 NLT).
- Submit to His will and obey Him.

As a result of trusting God, great things will happen. As a young man, I became a teacher in elementary school for two years. School was out for the summer in Baltimore. I was considering marrying a young lady God led me to at a church convention. I was shocked when I was drafted into the army. This threw a wrench in my plans. I really didn't know what I was going to do. I prayed and prayed. Around 1970, my church helped me become a conscientious objector. I refused to go into the military and bear arms. So I kept praying often and hard. I was told I could not work as an elementary teacher anymore. I had to take a salary cut for two years. I kept praying to God. He led me to the state employment agency. A day later the office called me back and notified me that there was an opening at a new childcare program. They were looking for a male teacher to work with very young children. This federal program focused on training parents to continue as the first and primary teachers of their children. The two-year program would also transform trainees into qualified childcare providers. The children ranged from infants to four-year-olds. This was a new concept at the time. A head teacher opening was available. The army approved of me taking the job. I knew God opened this door. I praised Him more and more. I trusted God to get me through this situation. I just didn't know how God would make it work for me.

This was, of course, a blessing in disguise. We had a supervisor who wrote the curriculum for the trainees and the children. She was hard and demanding, but she was fair. She also wanted the three head teachers to assist in writing new materials for the trainees and children. We needed to encourage the trainees to become certified childcare paraprofessionals. We were also supposed to guide them so that they would actually start their own childcare programs if they wanted. This was completely new to me.

God worked it out so that I received almost the same amount of salary as I had at my former teaching job. Thus, I could get married and live in an apartment in the county. Paying tithes and making offerings was a privilege I enjoyed even more.

My wife asked if it was possible for us move to Louisiana to be near her aging parents. Plus she had an older brother and younger sister there. I promised to move there if God helped me find a job and a brick home. I knew God would work everything out for His plan. I got the job, and we got the brick home after that.

Before moving to Louisiana, I decided to get a master's degree. I worked hard and earned good grades. It was mind-boggling to learn that my graduate counselor for my thesis was the husband of my supervisor at the center. He guided me, critiqued my paper, and finally approved my paper. That was another blessing that unfolded.

I got my master's degree in early childhood education months before we left for Louisiana. Several years later another door opened. Because of my degree and experience, I became an itinerant teacher for undergraduate students in my small town for two years. The students shared materials they made. They wrote practice proposals to start a daycare center. They got to better understand what it would take to run a quality daycare center. This was a blessing because we learned to trust God to work out everything according to His purpose.

Another blessing came my way during the summer right after moving to Louisiana. I became a consulting teacher at the same parent and child center I worked at before in Maryland. I was able to drive to Baltimore for three years during my summer break. This enabled me to visit my brothers and sisters. I also visited my sister who had recently moved to a place near Atlanta. It was great to be with her husband and three children. I was able to see her children while they were very young. They are now college grads and working at various organizations.

Among the senior trainees in Baltimore, two trainees became directors. I consulted with another graduating trainee to help her start and run her own home care center. God is able to do things you may not imagine are possible.

You can absolutely trust God to do what's best for you at the right time.

Trusting God enables you to have confidence and security (Psalm 37:3–9 NLT). You will have a rejoicing heart (Psalm 33:21), keep growing your personal relationship with Jesus, act on what you believe, and continue to grow and change. Keep walking with God. You won't fail.

If you want to please God, you must trust Him. Therefore, there won't be any worry, anxiety, or fear in your life that last. Just relax and trust Him to handle your burden. Don't lean on your understanding. Rather lean on Jesus in your heartache, burden, anger, confusion, and sorrow.

Even the devil doesn't know what to do with a believer who is willing to place others before themselves as a service to God. He cannot defeat obedient believers who have placed their trust in God firmly.

Trust God always. Talk to Him constantly. Remember His greatness, power, and promises. Understand His love and unique purpose for you. Serve Jesus, and share Him with others. Thank God for all He does for you and humankind every day.

God is daring you to trust Him in every situation. He wants you to be full of confidence and hope. Jesus actually came to give us sound minds, strong bodies, and healthy emotions. Entrust your life to His capable hands. He will do what He says once you give your situation over to Him. That confidence allows you to live your life boldly with joy and positive expectation. That growing confidence makes us comfortable and fearless so that we can do what God wants us to do. The stress, self-pity, pressure, worry, negative talking, and fear of failure all go away.

We should totally commit ourselves to God. When you trust God completely, you are placing yourself in His care. Keep refreshing that trust in God. He will tell you exactly what needs to be done as you follow the guidance of the Holy Spirit. Learn to give God total control of your life. That should be your lifelong goal.

Our trust should be unshakeable. We know God keeps His every promise. No matter what is happening around us, God will provide a way past the obstacles. He doesn't give up on us, so don't give up on God. He has places for you to go, people to affect, and things to do.

Victory is ensured when we trust God.

You are giving yourself totally to Him. This is another way to offer yourself to God as a sacrifice. We worship God because we totally trust Him.

"Therefore humble yourselves [demote, lower yourselves in your own estimation], under the mighty hand of God, that in due time He may exalt you, casting the whole of your care [all your anxieties, all your concerns, once and for all] on Him, for He cares for you affectionately and cares about you watchfully" (1 Peter 5:6, 7 AMPC).

Reflect Jesus Christ in Your Whole Life

The rest of the animal was also completely burned up. Our person becomes a sacrifice of worship through our daily experiences. Since you are redeemed your whole life is to be spent worshipping God. We can be consumed by the will of God. We are a whole burnt offering to God. He wants all of your dedication to be to Him.

The burnt offering was wholly consumed by fire on the altar. All sin is covered by the death of the Lord. Christians today will be tested and consumed by the true fire, the Holy Spirit. Your character and faith is to be proven. Since you trust God, everything will work out.

This offering represents Christ -or us- being completely devoted to Father God. He has given Himself for us as an offering and a sacrifice to God for a sweet savor (Ephesians 5: 2). As we accept Jesus as our burnt offering, we identify that He is our substitute. He was always in complete submission to the Father. We also are suppose to completely submit our will and desires to God.

Jesus Christ is the center of our offerings. As we offer our self to God, we are forgiven and reconciled back to God only because of Jesus. Jesus Christ also becomes our sin offering as we accept the perfect righteous death He offered. This restores our relationship with God the Father.

Jesus's feelings, thoughts, and activities-his total life- were placed in submission to God. When the offerors yields themselves to God, then their lives are sweet and satisfying to the Lord. God is satisfied because the offerors have met His requirement by the righteous way they live their lives. Thus, the offering is accepted.

15. Be Transformed to Become like Jesus

After Trusting God

"May your whole spirit, soul, and body be kept blameless at the coming of our Lord" (1 Thessalonians 5:23).

"Present yourselves to God as those alive from the dead, and your members as instruments of righteousness to God" (Romans 6:13b NASB).

"But if the Spirit of Him who raised Jesus from the dead will also give life to your mortal bodies through His Spirit who dwells in you … If you are living according to the flesh, you must die, but if by the Spirit you are putting to death the deeds of the body, you will live" (Romans 8:11, 13).

Decide to offer your body as the temple. "Do you not know that your body is a temple of the Holy Spirit who is in you, whom you have from God, and that you are not your own. For you have been bought with a price; therefore glorify God in your body" (1 Corinthians 6:19–20 NASB).

God wants to transform your body. Being transformed into the image of Jesus is our real goal in life (2 Corinthians 3:18 The Message). "Our life is gradually becoming brighter and brighter and more beautiful as God enters our lives and we become more like him." You can trust God to transform us into the image of Christ. The Spirit will do this through His Word.

You must start with your mind. To live in accordance with the Spirit, you must have your mind set on what the Spirit desires. So if your mind is governed by the Spirit, you will have life and peace (Romans 8:5–7). He will transform us from inside out. Our victory comes through a renewed mind and heart. It's a process of becoming more like Christ. This is a spiritual rebirth. This starts when we receive salvation after we are forgiven and justified. Our God isn't finished with anyone. He is drawing us to Himself, and He is transforming us as we trust Him more and more. He wants us to receive His grace and new life every moment of every day.

"God's purpose in choosing believers for Himself is so that they declare His praises before others. Believers should live so that their heavenly Father's qualities are evident in their lives. We are to serve as witnesses of the glory and grace of God, who called them out of darkness into His marvelous light" (1 Peter 2:9). We are to bear witness to the nature and character of Christ and His coming kingdom. We are to offer our bodies to him as instruments of righteousness.

You are a new creation in Christ. The life of Jesus is to be revealed in our actions. As you lay aside the old self, you are brought to life in the Spirit. We have been set free to overcome sin, and we have become slaves to God. Keep in mind that we are fighting society, Satan, and ourselves. All three resist the Holy Spirit's desires and guidance. This ongoing struggle keeps us from submitting to the will of God.

Live your new life boldly. Trust God completely.

Paul was talking about the most important change we will ever experience—the time when we trade our sinful lives for salvation in Christ (2 Corinthians 5:17 AMPC).

You are fighting the world, Satan, and yourself. There is an ongoing struggle between your human nature and Jesus's divine nature within you. Use the armor of God to stand firm.

This means you are submitting to Christ's reign in your life every day. We, the people of God, are striving to come fully under Jesus's rule. Jesus is Lord and Savior now. He is reigning. However, that real kingdom is now hidden. The full effects of His reign are not shown in this evil world. When Christ returns, the reality of the kingdom will be made fully obvious. Uncover the truth and reality of who Jesus is and what He has accomplished. We want to serve Jesus now so that we can serve Him forever in our new glorified bodies. This is the great hope we have.

We must move into a new way of thinking and acting. Your destiny is to change and look forward. God can transform every part of your life when you finally see the new possibilities. You should desire to become whole and balanced in your spiritual health (love, trust, and faith), in your physical health (body care), in your relationships (family, friends, coworkers, enemies), in your mental and emotional health, and in your finances.

Be a person who sees and understands the truth of God. Be a person who listens to and obeys God. Be a person who lives to keep a close relationship with God and loves his or her fellow man. Be a person who uses his or her great support system—God.

Keep trusting Jesus to be filled up with Him. You're transforming into a new person. You are becoming what God created you to be. God wants you to become like Him in character and mind. Ask God to help you be better in planning, evaluating, designing, creating, and problem-solving.

God adores you for giving all your life to Him. God is pleased to see you adopting the stature and fullness of Jesus Christ. Remember God is ready to help you. He delights in your dedication and trust.

As you give control to God, you are changing to become more like Jesus Christ. This is the ultimate offering you make to God.

"Or don't you realize that your body is a sacred place, the place of the Holy Spirit? Don't you see that you can't live however you please, squandering what God paid such a high price for? The physical, part of you is not some piece of property belonging to the spiritual part of you. God owns the whole works. So let people see God in and through you" (1 Corinthians 6:19, 20 The Message).

"For our citizenship is in heaven, from which also we eagerly wait for a Savior, the Lord Jesus Christ: who will transform the body of our humble state into conformity with the body of His glory, by the exertion of the power that He has even to subject all things to Himself" (Philippians 3:20–21 NASB).

16. Be a Priest for the Gospel

"But you shall be named the priest of the LORD, They shall call you the servants of our God" (Isaiah 61:6a NKJV).

"To be a minister of Christ Jesus to the Gentiles. He gave me the priestly duty of proclaiming the gospel of God, so that the Gentiles might become an offering acceptable to God, sanctified by the Holy Spirit" (Romans 15:16).

"Present yourselves as building stones for the construction of a sanctuary vibrant with life, in which you'll serve as holy priest offering Christ approved lives up to God" (1 Peter 2:5 The Message).

"For every high priest is appointed to offer both gifts and sacrifices; so it is necessary that this high priest also have something to offer" (Hebrews 8:3 NASB)

A priest is also called a minister, and a minister is called a priest too. So says Martin Luther, a Protestant Reformer. If you are a follower of Jesus Christ, you are a minister. All believers and Christ followers are ministers. We minister to those in the church and to others around us.

We are a holy people who offer spiritual sacrifices through Jesus Christ. We are a church of priests (1 Peter 2:4–5 The Message). We are called the priesthood of all believers because of our relationship with God through Jesus Christ.

As ministers, we have been given gifts and talents to serve others. We are charged with using the ones given to us with zeal. Be generous as well. First Peter 4:10–11 mentions the gifts of speaking and helping others. Everything we do is to bring glory to God through Jesus Christ. We are not called to be bystanders. Rather God wants us to be volunteers. Ephesians 4:7–15 tells us that Christ gives each one of us a gift through His generosity. He gave gifts to the apostles, the prophets, the evangelists, the pastors, and the teachers to equip His people for service. He wants us to become mature members and grow into His fullness. Our acts of ministry will unite us. We are to stir up love and perform good works. We are to submit to the ministry. Every member belongs to the community. Do what you know how to do. Even try something new. Above all, be involved in the work of God.[22]

I'm not talking about ordained pastors, elders, and preachers called to directly serve the church. They have a unique set of skills, responsibilities, and rewards as shepherds of God's sheep.

Our servant mind-set is different. We should be prepared to share our great relationship with God. We know God because of Bible study, prayer, and living faith. A priest is ready to teach and share why he has so much hope in Jesus. We must also have a sincere desire to help others. A minister also loves his neighbors and wants them to love one another. You are a source of encouragement for those who need to see God as He really is— compassionate, merciful, slow to anger, faithful, loving, and forgiving. Some just need a few positive words. Some may just need a reminder that God loves them and has a plan for them. You confirm with your whole being that Jesus is worthy of our praise, love, and trust. When you encourage others to return to God and to keep trusting Him, you are

---

[22] Pastor Mike Booze, "Acts 11:19–26—Everyone's Commission," Faith Community in Shreveport, LA.

being a priest. We are meant to help one another. You are supposed to act with humility.

A. Share the Gospel Using Spiritual CPR

Acts 11:19–26 tells of what believers did after they were driven from Jerusalem. Acts 8:1, 4 says they went "on their way," sharing the good news.

Matthew 28:19–20 tells us to share the gospel. This is everyone's commission! We make the gospel part of our everyday lives and talk about it with the people in our lives. We don't have to *preach* to them. We just have talk to them. As you go about sharing Jesus, provide the spiritual CPR needed.

> *Cultivate* relationships with the unchurched. Visit with them over coffee. Invite them to dinner. Have an evangelism at a barbecue. Everyone needs to feel the love of God.
>
> *Plant* the gospel. Converse with people about their beliefs and yours. Answer questions about church and other things. Offer to pray for them.
>
> *Reap.* Invite them! Ask if they would like to visit your life group. Would they like to come to your church? Pick them up, and bring them. Introduce them to others. Take them to dinner after church and process the experience. Invite them again for next week.

Unnamed men from Cyprus began to share the gospel with Greeks. They could be anybody or everybody. The Lord was pleased that ordinary members now carried the gospel to their friends, neighbors, and family.

How can we be involved in everybody's commission? First, we must offer prayers. Pray for the lost and unchurched people. Let them know you pray for them. Second, care for others. Show acts of service and kindness for them. Show hospitality.[23]

Through a series of Bible studies, Russell Duke revealed that we believers are priest (ministers) who can share the gospel and love of Christ informally as the opportunity comes up.

A priest has several functions we should be aware of today.

Your personal conduct is the key to your influence and involvement. You are called to live a holy life. You have been selected for God's purpose and glory.

Seek to make a positive impact on people around you. Be present and involved in the lives of those you have contact with. Remember God loves each one of them. They are in the image of God. Listen to what makes them happy and sad. Then you'll know what to pray about and what to do.

Encourage others to give their lives to God as sacrifices. This book presents five offerings that Israel gave. (Review part three in this book.) We must confess our sins daily. We must seek to live peaceful lives with others, and we have to fix situations when we trespass against others. Do good works for others. Give your heart, soul, mind, and strength completely to Him. Seek to have a deeper relationship with God. These five strategies encourage God to keep revealing Himself more and more to you.

Model Jesus's way of life within your personal behavior. The Holy Spirit leads and guides as you listen.

Express your sincere care and concern for others. Be ready to share your gospel story with friends and those in your family, your workplace, and your neighborhood. Ask God to help you identify the person in your life who needs to hear the good news of Jesus. As you share, Jesus will overflow into the lives of those around us.

---

[23] Pastor Mike Booze, "The Ministry of All Believers," Faith Community in Shreveport, LA, February 28, 2016.

Celebrate Jesus as the spiritual fulfillment of Israel's Sabbath and festivals.

Jesus is the center of Sabbath and festivals. He is the real light of those holy days. He is far greater than the symbols themselves. Jesus, the Lord of the Sabbath and the Messiah, wants us to take time to relate to Him. We can find peace between us and our creator (Romans 5:1). He is our Sabbath peace. Jesus is our eternal rest and redemption.

Jesus is the Passover Lamb. He became the sin offering when He shed His blood for humankind (John 1:29). His sacrifice enables us to be sanctified and redeemed in the eyes of the Father. We need God's forgiveness, mercy, and grace. We now have a relationship and a future with Him because of Jesus's blood.

The Feast of Unleavened Bread reveals our need to cleanse our hearts. Confess your sin so that you are not prevented from having an intimate relationship with the Lord. The Messiah can cleanse our lives of sin. Get sin out of your life. God forgives sin. He is the bread of life. Firstfruits shows that Jesus was first resurrected and accepted by God. Father God was pleased and delighted to make Jesus the first one who was resurrected and ascended to Him. We then received "the firstfruits of the Spirit" (Romans 8:23 NLT), and we become a kind of firstfruits among His new creation (James 1:18) to live lives dedicated to the Lord.

Pentecost shows the outpouring of the Holy Spirit to the whole world. We now have help in living lives pleasing to God through Jesus Christ. We are ready to proclaim the good news to those around us.

Trumpets ultimately point to the gathering of the body of the Messiah to meet the Lord (1 Corinthians 15:51–52; 1 Thessalonians 4:16–18). Expecting Jesus to return motivates us to live lives of service. God is gathering His people. We also must seek to lead people to Jesus while there is time. His gift of faith will assure a new life. The Holy Spirit is available to those who believe in Jesus.[24]

---

[24] Russell Duke, assistant professor of theology, "Several Functions of Priest," Ambassador College, Shreveport, LA, December 14, 1991.

The Day of Atonement (Yom Kippur) points out that we are fallen creatures without the grace, mercy, and atonement of God in the Messiah. We need humble hearts and the Jesus's blood sacrifice in order to be acceptable to God. Then our relationship is restored with God. The gathering of Israel is coming. The gathering of believers is also coming.

The Feast of Tabernacles (Feast of Booths) shows Jesus is the living water and the light. The Holy Spirit is poured out to those who trust and believe in Him. There is true security in God. All nations will gather to glorify Jesus, the King of Kings and Lord of Lords. He already is our King and Lord.

In Hanukkah (Feast of Dedication), Jesus modelled a life dedicated to the Father. He is the light of the world. Faith in Jesus is the real victory. He cleanses us from our sins so that we might be a sacred temple for holy worship to the glory of God. Dedicate yourself to the service of the divine King. We are to serve him. God gives victory to His people.

The Feast of Purim shows God is faithful to His promises to Israel and the world of believers. Esther repented and pleaded to the king on behalf of her people's welfare, and the Jewish people were saved from extinction once again. God loves everybody. Jesus's return will be a blessing to all people. Believers know that the gospel is the only way the Jewish people (and all people) will be saved from judgment. So we must warn others and help them repent and believe in Jesus.[25]

Priest will certainly talk about and actually obey the commands of Jesus. Priests also have duties and responsibilities to perform.

You proclaim the gospel of God. This is done by your life and your testimony. You use your gifts to minister (serve) to others. When God blesses you, He wants you to share with those in need. God has equipped you for works of service. What is the best thing you do? Our overall

---

[25] Sam Nadler, *The Messiah of the Feast of Israel* (Charlotte: Word of Messiah Ministries, 2010), 26–27, 56–57, 102, 111, 120, 144, 152, 160, 201–5.

purpose is to help people to mature and better reflect Jesus. This is how we glorify and honor God.

As God begins to open your mind and heart, do not become proud, high-minded, bigheaded, or arrogant (Proverbs 6:16 NKJV). God hates that attitude. Any success you are a part of is because you are learning to better yield to God and trust Him. Remember God is working through you. He'll guide you so that you know when to share, where to share, and how to share the gospel. Just be ready and available.

You cannot be of true service to God unless you continually confess your sins to Him. Ask for forgiveness, and always surrender yourself to the Lord (Psalm 32:1–5 NLT). Our sins disappear then. God is ready to forgive your sins.

Present yourself as a living spiritual sacrifice to God. He wants all of you. This book outlines the areas in your life that enable you to give your heart, soul, mind, and strength to the service of God (Luke 10:27 NLT). This keeps your whole life going in the right direction and allows you to keep that close relationship with God.[26] Since you are the temple and priest of God, you are responsible for offering acceptable spiritual sacrifices.

Keep demonstrating the fact that our relationship with God is of prime importance. He desires a close relationship with you. Take the time to meet one-on-one with God. Take the time to pray or talk to God. Read the Word, and really hear God. In your humility you will trust Him to complete His plan for you and others.

Show mercy and compassion toward others (Psalm 103:8–10, 13–14). Then God will also show you mercy.

Keep the commands of God. This shows that you really love Him.

---

[26] [29] Russell Duke, assistant professor of theology, "Duties and Rules of a Priest Today," Ambassador College, Shreveport, LA, December 21, 1991.

Offer your gifts and talents to serve and help others and the church. Determine what your talents are, and use them to serve others. By being aware of others' talents, you can also encourage them to serve others (Hebrews 5:1–3, 8:2–3) as needs are identified. But you know you can ask God to guide you and others. Be aware that people will seek you because you are a priest (minister) of God (Nehemiah 12:27). Stay humble! You are being tested. Are you going to take the credit yourself or give it to God? Remember that God is working through you for a purpose. The underlying purpose of the church is "to prepare God's people for works of service, so that the body of Christ may be built up" (Ephesians 4:12–13).

Promote reconciliation to God as best as you can. Suggest to people ways to return to God (Joel 2:12–13).

Give suitable support to the pastor, church leaders, and people of God. Share the good news with those who show interest in Jesus Christ. Bind up the brokenhearted. Proclaim liberty to the captives. Pray for the healing of needy people.[27]

God has plans for you. Keep changing to be a better reflection of Jesus. Be the minister of service God wants you to be. We shall become more like Christ. We shall become priests and kings in the kingdom of God.

"But you are a chosen people, a royal priesthood, a holy nation, God's special possession, that you may declare the praises of him who called you out of darkness into his wonderful light" (1 Peter 2:9).

"I delight greatly in the LORD; my soul rejoices in my God. For he has clothed me with garments of salvation and arrayed me in a robe of his righteousness" (Isaiah 61:10a).

"They will be called the Holy People, the Redeemed of the LORD; and you will be called Sought After, the City No Longer Deserted" (Isaiah 62:12).

---

[27] Russell Duke, assistant professor of theology, "Duties of a Priest Today," Ambassador College, Shreveport, LA, December 21, 1991.

CHAPTER FOUR

Do Good Deeds to Others

Meal Offering / Grain Offering

The Meal Offering is the fourth sacrifice that Israel made to God. This also is a freewill or voluntary offering like the burnt offering. It was the only offering where blood was not involved. It also was a way to give oneself completely to God. This is something we can do using the fruit of the ground. This speaks of growing grains to make flour.

At times three offerings were made at once. The Burnt Offering was made first. Then comes the Meal Offering. Following the Meal Offering came the Peace Offering.

The offering shows the recognition of God's blessing in the harvest of a society based largely on farming. The small portion of the grain was another expression of devotion.

The meal offering required no shedding of blood and had nothing to do with atonement for sin, our trespass or our consecration to the Lord.

It dealt with presenting our loving deeds for others in a way that would please God.

It was a voluntary meal offering made of fine flour. Your grain offering was made up of fine flour, frankincense, and oil. Salt was dashed on it for flavor. Each ingredient has a meaning. No leaven allowed in the bread because it symbolizes sin and corruption (1 Corinthians 5: 7). Leaven was a type of weakness of our sinful human flesh. No honey was added because it smells badly when burned in the fire.

The grain offering could be made in three ways. The first way is the fine flour with oil and frankincense. The second type of meal offering was the cake /wafer. The fine flour was mixed with oil and baked as wafers. No leaven or yeast could be used. The third way to offer a grain offering was with crashed heads of new corn grain roasted by fire. Then, it was beaten out of the ears or heads to be sacrificed.

Procedure of Offering (Leviticus 2: 1-16 The Message)

The meal offering had to follow specific procedures only by the priest. The part offered by the priest was totally consumed with fire for a sweet smelling savor. Only a portion of the offering was burned on the altar. The remainder went to the priest. Presenting the meal offering, the priest brought it in the gold or silver dish in which it had been prepared. Then he transferred it to a holy vessel, putting it and frankincense on it. Standing at the south corner of the altar, he took a 'handful that was to be burned, put it in another vessel, laid some of the frankincense on it, carried it to the top of the altar, salted it, and placed it on the fire. The priest could only offer the meal offering for it to be accepted. If a stranger, an unbeliever, or unsaved person offered the meal offering, it would be for nothing and not be accepted.

Let's see how the ingredients reflect our endurance to serve, being tested, involving The Holy Spirit, and deepening our fellowship with God. Jesus Christ offered Himself perfectly to The Father. The fine flour is our keep serving and doing well in spite of the hardness of our hearts. We do great activities for a while, and then we get tired of doing these acts of goodness (Galatians 6: 9-10). We tend to be up and down. But Jesus shows the same perfect character always. The oil is the Holy Spirit being poured on us. When we are baptized, we receive the gift of the Holy Spirit, to lead, guide, and strengthen us as we go through difficult trials and temptations. He is constantly instructing us in the way of Jesus. He brings to our mind verses and scripture that helps us in situations. That's why reading and studying the Word is so important. Jesus Christ used that same power of the Holy Spirit effectively when given an unmeasured amount. The frankincense represented a delightful fragrance and savor when God is pleased with you. The aroma of Jesus's life is great. You don't know how dedicated you are until your faith is tried in fire. You will have to under go trails and test to see where you are in obedience and trust in God. God then sees if you are for real. Jesus offering Himself doing those very hard times became even more fragrant and precious to God. Finally, salt was added to give flavor. Our speech and conduct should be in good flavor. We should be the salt of the earth. Salt in our lives reminds us to stay in the way and not return to the old nature. God wants you to endure to the end. Salt is a preservative as well. God wants us to remember His eternal covenant with you.

The meal offering was always offered with the burnt offering. This underlined that service to man without giving devotion to God is not an acceptable offering (Luke 14: 26). God always comes first.

It is the offering of the fruit of your labor instead of an animal's life. This points to our own efforts, labor, good works of our hands. It shows a natural product that was created by the effort of humankind. We are created unto good works. Of course, we know our good works don't justify us before God. Only the sinless blood of Jesus justifies you before God. Our so called righteousness is considered as fifthly rags by God. We should not put any confidence in the flesh (Philippians 3:3).

God wants you to put to death whatever belongs to your earthly nature. Various translations of Galatians 5: 16-17 express our nature as "desires of the flesh" (NLT) (NASB), "the works of the flesh" (NKJV), "trying to get your own way all the time"(The Message), and desires of the sinful nature"

(NIV). "The acts of the sinful nature are obvious". They are listed in verses 19, 20, 21. Those that live like this will not inherit the kingdom of God (verse 21b). This sinful nature is contrary to the Holy Spirit.

God tells us to rather live by the Spirit. Believers are actively crucifying the sinful nature with its passions and desires. We seek to live by the Spirit showing its fruits of love, peace, patience, kindness, goodness, faithfulness, gentleness and self-control (Galatians 5: 22,23,24).

Those who belong to Christ Jesus are putting on the new self. It is being renewed in the image of Christ (Colossians 2: 5-10). God wants you to love him. "Do your best to present yourself to God as one approved, a workman who does not feel ashamed and who correctly handles the word of truth" (2 Timothy 2: 15).

So we must do good with a right attitude and motivation from the heart and mind. Do good to really help others in need. We don't do good to be seen as holy, generous, and outstanding by others. Don't give money and material things to get favors for position and authority, or to be in the inner circle of the ministry. God looks at the heart of people to see if they act out of love and concern. Since Jesus is in us, His love will flow from Him to you to others. This brings us to a closer relationship to God.

Our good deeds of love should meet several standards of conduct. There is suppose to be no sin in your life. God wants us to live with the unleavened bread of sincerity and truth. Your deeds must be free of the weakness that is from our sinful carnal human nature. Our good deeds must give honor and glory to God. You are created to do good works which God prepared in advance for us to do. When you do something right and good, thank God. The receiver will thank God because of what you did.

Our good deeds need to be tried by the fire of sincerity and truth. It must be brought to Jesus and tested. The offering reveals, in type, a sweet savor or pleasing offering acceptable to God in the form of love for man fulfilling the second commandment which says "you shall love your neighbor as yourself" (Matthew 22: 39).

Prayer for others is a great way to do something good. Pray for your family (mates, children, brothers and sisters, in-laws), pastor, local church members, government authorities, those who don't know Jesus, other believers, coworkers, laborers in the harvest, and the officials of your town or city.

You must first devote yourself completely to God. Cain's offering of the fruit without a burnt offering was not acceptable to God. He should have offered an animal first. Abel did offer an animal sacrifice to God.

All the aspects of offering good deeds should reflect Jesus's perfect life and sacrifice. He has set the example for us. He did what he could for the sick, poor, hungry, brokenhearted, blind, and the captive. God wants you to care for those in need and are suffering, starting with those close to you. There is also a spiritual fulfillment to the mission you and Jesus are on: preach the good news to the poor and unbelievers; proclaim freedom for the prisoners of fear, worry, sin; recover the sight of the blind; and release the oppressed (Luke 4: 18-19 NKJV).

We are charged to do good works to glorify Father God and follow Jesus's example. As we go through each day, our focus should be on the glory of God. "Let your light shine before others, that they may see your good deeds and glorify your Father in heaven" (Matthew 5: 16). We should turn people's attention back to God. Our labor of love brings rewards. We will be rewarded for good works done in obedience to God, according to His power, and for His glory"

We must remember that our salvation comes from what Jesus has done. It is not from what you do.

Our good works should be fueled from believing and receiving Jesus's gift. The desire to serve happens because Christ lives in us. These good deeds are for God. Through the Holy Spirit, Christ gets to do what he wants to do. As you are being lead by the Spirit, others will see the fruits of your ways.

Be very careful when others see how well you are using the gifts of the Holy Spirit. They want to give you all the credit and convince you that you did it alone. This is a test! Remind those who are giving you all this praise that God deserves the glory not you. God gave you the abilities to get it done.

The unleavened bread of sincerity and truth also can remind us of the broken body of Jesus at the communion service. Jesus is the bread of life. He is the center of our salvation and the reason we are given grace freely.

"And so, dear brothers, I plead with you to give your bodies to God. Let them be a living sacrifice, holy- the kind he can accept. When you think of what he has done for you, is this too much to ask?" (Romans 12:1 TLB).

CHAPTER FIVE

Remain in Christ and Fellowship with Father God

Peace Offering / Fellowship Offering

The fifth and final sacrifice is the peace offering. It is also called the fellowship offering. This is a voluntary act of worship. It is an expression of thanks or gratitude to God for His bounties and mercies. The Israelites enjoyed success and prosperity for individuals and/or the nation. They want to thank God for enjoying what God has provided. They were reminded of how near God was. The offerors also are reminded of the protection God gives when adversity (problems) threatens to take his mind off God. They are glad God is there to refocus them. These people just want to thank God for the great things He has provided. Those individuals have a great sense of peace and gratitude.

The fellowship offering seems to center on the simple desire to thank God for the enjoyment of his provisions. He wants to make supplication for God to keep on providing for him.

It expressed peace and fellowship between the offeror and God. It was restoring the communion with God. This relationship was very important to the individual. This is even more important to God than the things you do. Abiding in the love of God is the essence of our relationship.

The peace offering had nothing to do with sin. Rather the offerors were thanking God, making a vow because they survived a life of threatening crises, or he was giving a freewill offering.

It came last when there was a series of offerings made. So the offeror would give a burnt offering, alone with meal offering and then a peace (thanksgiving and fellowship) offering.

Making a peace offering would imply that you reject the world and embrace the cross.

Real Christians remain in fellowship with Jesus and the body of fellow brothers and sister in Christ. Keep on abiding in Christ and His Word. Keep on delighting in God. Keep on honoring God.

Procedure of Offering (Leviticus 7: 11-16)

The peace offering was a feast of love and joy of His people showing the honor of dwelling in the house and family of the Lord. This also revealed the joy of His people before Him.

A bull, cow, lamb, or goat without a defect would be used. It could be male or female. The offeror placed his hands on the animal and killed it. The Priest would then cut off the fatty portions (fat covering the inner parts) to be burnt. This is God's portion. The Priest would sprinkle the blood around the altar. Just a representative of the offering was burnt on the altar. Only the internal organs were burnt up as a food offering. The Priest received the breast and the right thigh of the animal as his portion. The offerors were given much of the meat so they could have a meal of celebration with their families. If it was a thanksgiving offering, all the remainder had to be eaten on the same day. Nothing was left.

It was the only offering in which the offeror shared the meat, the unleavened bread, and wine that's drunk. It was like a sacrificial meal. "since the Peace offering was the only sacrifice the Israelite could eat, every time he wanted to eat meat for dinner, he had to offer a Peace Offering".

The offeror and their family ate the physical food of the peace offering. It was a symbol that they spiritually fed with the mercies of God. This also meant being satisfied with the fullness of joy in the presence of the Lord (Psalm 16:11).

All is well since there is a peaceful relationship between the Lord and the person. God is no longer angry with the offeror. God's favor is with him now. The peace of knowing you are forgiven is really great and refreshing. You now have access to God. Thus, you want to share that close relationship with the priest and your family as you eat the meal of celebration.

This offering always came last when offered with other kinds of offerings.

Making a peace offering has two parts: 1) making peace with God by getting right by confessing our sins, and 2) offering to have fellowship with God over our fellowship with the world.

We are to give up anything that prevents us from having fellowship with God.

The peace offering has to do with our communion with Father God, the Priest (Jesus Christ), and family of believers.

You have the chance to thank God by giving a thanksgiving offering to Him. God tells you to offer a sacrifice of thanksgiving (Psalm 50:23, Colossians 3:15). When you give a thanksgiving offering, you honor God. You also, make a covenant with Him. That covenant is to become a new person. You are to bury the old you. Having a thankful spirit, releases the supernatural power of God in your life. God sees you appreciate Him. You even reflect the presence of the Holy Spirit in your life. When you pray, start with praising and thanking God. A thankful person gives effective prayers. Spirit - filled people are thankful people.

There are so many reasons to thank God. They are numberless. After all, we are alive and well. God has unfailing love for you that endures forever. He has done and is doing so many wonderful deeds for humanity. God is good. He is very merciful. God is very compassionate. He is slow to anger and forgives us of our sin. God is our source of peace, joy, and hope. These are only a few reasons we have to thank the awesome, powerful, and loving God. The rewards for being thankful will be further explained in the section 10. Be Thankful to God and Neighbor".

This offering shows Christ is our peace offering (Ephesians 2: 12,18 NLT). Jesus is our source of real and true peace of mind. Once you recognize the awesome sacrifice of Jesus, you automatically commune with God. You have a sense of closeness and oneness with Jesus Christ. You seek to give your whole life to God. You are striving to put Him first always. You seek to be in His presence more and more. You want to know Jesus and share the confidence you receive. You are at peace and full of joy because of God. This is fun and exciting as God moves you to ways to better relate to Him.

He wants that deeper and better relationship with you always. He wants it to keep growing stronger. He seeks to reveal more and more of his nature and character to you.

Prayer is one way to communion with God. This is your chance to have a great one-on-one conversation with the perfect, holy, righteous, and loving God of the universe. You get to openly and sincerely talk to God. Your reverence for Him comes out as you praise and thank Him. This act allows you to bring Him glory. We do everything we can to satisfy God. We get to know God. Thus love Him. Thus obey Him. Thus worship Him. We can conform our lives to His will and His ways. We get to advance His kingdom. Plus, you can share anything and everything with Him. You have the chance to pray for those in need, the sick, the lost, those who have problems. You have a chance to request help for family, friends, church, missionaries, government authorities, and countries. Praying to

God strengthens your relationship, and it becomes easier to share what's happening in your life with Him.

Studying the Word of God also provides a means to communing with God. As you read and study the Word, good thoughts come to you. You also gain an awareness of what not to think, say, and do. It confirms what you know about God, the disciples, prophets, and Jesus Himself. Your learning corrects your wrong understanding. You get to see the same truth taught by different people in different times. God reveals simple and complex understandings to you. God tells you what you need to know about yourself, about Him, about eternal life, and about the gospel, and about a close relationship with Jesus. Holy Spirit will show what you must know at the moment in your life. The book of John, Romans 8, Ephesians 1-3 are good places to start and deepen your Bible study. This is why studying your Bible is so important as a way to relate to God. The Holy Spirit will guide in all of this.

Actually, doing with God as He directs you is the greatest fellowship and communion. You have a common interest and purpose at a certain time and place. As you talk to others to encourage them, or work in the mission God gave you, it becomes satisfying. Listening to a non-believing friend tell you about personal problems may give you goose-bumps as Holy Spirit tells you how to begin to turn him to Jesus. You can say what God inspires you to say when the person ask, "How can God help me?" or "Why won't God help me?" There are countless moments when you and God are connected. These are the great moments when God and you act as one. This glorifies God. He is very pleased with this.

Our fellowship is with the Father and with His Son, Jesus Christ is the most important thing we can have (1 Corinthians 1:9, 2 Corinthians 13: 14 NKJV). This happens when God forgives us of our sin and then bring us into a closer relationship with Him. Remain in fellowship with Father God, Jesus Christ God, the Holy Spirit. Your brothers and sisters in Christ also share a desire to commune with God as a group. We have the same holy Father, Son of God, and Holy Spirit in our hearts. Jesus must be the center of our lives. So as we actually listen and learn from Jesus, our dedication and love for Him grows stronger. Talking with Jesus is a great way to keep our trust strong. We know He is working to help us handle any situation we face.

Our real goal is to know Jesus better. Thus, we want to reflect his values and ways in our lives.

Salvation is the common interest that you and God share. God wants to give you eternal life and you want to receive eternal life. God gives eternal life the moment you believe Jesus is His son. When you accept Christ as your Savior, you then possess eternal life. God is very interested in you. He has been working so we will be with Him forever and ever. You now have eternal life since Jesus lives in you through the Holy Spirit (1 John 5: 11-13). Your fellowship and communion with Jesus assures you will spend eternity with Him. It's a matter of how great your rewards and inheritance will be.

In summary, these five offerings were thoughtfully created to keep the Savior in the center our lives within the old covenant and Jesus the center of the new covenant today. You must realize you need your sins forgiven daily. You need to be reconciled to Father God. You are supposed to treat your fellow man with love and respect. You need to give your life totally to God. You need to keep a close relationship with God. Each has its part. All of these are only possible because of the shed blood of Jesus and His resurrection. Having communion is a sign that we remain in Christ. If you want to live in an intimate relationship with the Lord, live a life illuminated by God's Word. Be in the realm of truth. Applying His truth to our lives is very practical. This is the deep desire to be in the presence of God.

These devotions (offerings) to God encourages Him to reveal more of His character to you. He wants you to be like Him. He will keep coming to you showing how deep His love is.

When Aaron, the Priest, sought to present the people to God, he offered three sacrifices: the sin offering, the burnt offering, and the fellowship offering. God wants us to always repent and ask for forgiveness, devote our entire life to Him, and seek a closer fellowship type relationship with Jesus. When Aaron did this, God came as the glory of the LORD (Leviticus 9: 22). God accepted their sacrifices. As believers of Jesus, God accepts us and makes his presence known. We know God is always with us and will not forsake us. We see more of what God is really like in perfect love.

The new covenant enables us to obtain forgiveness that does not involve physical sacrifices at all. The book of Jonah tells of an entire community condemned to destruction that was forgiven when they simply repented and fasted, without ever offering any physical sacrifice, blood or otherwise (Jonah 3: 8-10).

Likewise, we are forgiven of our sins by simply repenting and asking God to forgive us. He is ready to forgive.

"And so, dear brothers and sisters, I plead with you to give your bodies to God because of all he has done for you. Let them be a living and holy sacrifice- the kind he find acceptable (Romans 12: 1 NLT.)

CHAPTER SIX

Stay Hot for God

Keep the Fire Burning

"The fire on the altar shall be kept burning on it. It shall not go out, but the priest shall burn wood on it every morning; and he shall lay out the burnt offering on it, and offer up in smoke the fat portions of the peace offering on it. Fire shall be kept burning continually on the altar, it is not to go out" (Leviticus 6: 12-13 NASB)

The fire that was needed to burn the flesh was kept outside the camp or tabernacle. "For the bodies of those animals whose blood is brought into the holy place by the high priest as an offering for sin, are burned outside the camp. Therefore, Jesus also, that He might sanctify the people through His own blood, suffered outside the gate. So, let us go out to him outside the camp, bearing His reproach. For here we do not have a lasting city, but we are seeking the city which is to come." (Hebrew 13: 11-14 NASB)

To make the animal offerings, the priest had to chose a clean place for the ceremony. It was outside the camp and burned in a wood fire on the ash heap (Leviticus 4: 10-12).

A continual fire on the altar was commanded by God. The fire must be burning. Dr. John E. Montgomery liken fire burning being stoked to two concepts. First, there is the ongoing forgiveness of God. He is always ready to forgive (Psalm 86: 5). We can go to God anytime. You know God is always ready when you are sincere. It doesn't matter what the failure, shortcoming, or wrong doing might be. Confess your sins to God. Be ready to show someone else that same way of forgiveness.

The second concept liken to keeping the fire burning is the need for continual consequences. We should be constantly consecrated to God. We are to stay close to God. Keep your fire of passion for God strong. People at times are going to see if the fire in your soul is still burning. Keep your love and zeal going. First, you are going to have to be diligent and constantly alert to the level of flame of the fire. Honor God's promises in His Word. Next, you must know to feed the fire. A physical fire doesn't need green or wet wood. A wrong harsh word to someone can cause the fire of love to burn out. Flames must continue to grow. Feed the fire with the Word of God. Keep your Bible study, prayer habit, and meditation going. Finally, don't let the fire go too low. Rather, you must keep a good level going. Thus, be ready to fan the fire[28].

Don't lose your first love. Keep loving God and your fellowman like you suppose to. Keep putting God above anything or anyone: family and friends, job and careers, or money and power. Don't put up with sin in your life as you keep repenting. Keep that passion for the lost or unbelievers. Seek to be a witness to others for Jesus.

God wants you to fight against anything that keeps you from being passionate and fully focused on Jesus Christ. Following His plan- in His strength- is the way to peace, joy, and contentment in life.

---

[28] Pastor Dr. John Montgomery, "Keep the Offering Fire Constantly Burning", Greater King David Baptist Church' Baton Rouge, LA, FM Radio 88.1, August 1, 2018.

In summary, our fire is the Word of God. Feed the fire with effective prayers. Keep the level of your fire going steady by worshipping God with all your heart Remain motivated. Stay compassionate, and preach the gospel to the world. Everyone should see that zeal you possess because you are serving Him and the church. Keep overcoming and growing. Keep that first love going. Keep your love for God burning.

CONTINUE BEING A DELIGHT TO GOD

In this book, you are challenged to be a total spiritual sacrifice to God. He makes it clear that anything less than your best will not be acceptable. Who you are in Christ shows that you desire to give every part of your life to God.

God works with dedication to make you more aware that your relationship with Him is so important. He has always wanted a close relationship with you. Glorifying God is what your life should be about. God is very pleased when you devote your life to Him.

God chose Israel to be a holy nation. He also called the believers and saints of God to keep the holiness He granted by His grace. We are to remember all Christ has already done and thus live quite different from the surrounding world. We, too, are supposed to impact the world with the truth of God—the way of love. That responsibility has been entrusted to the church (Exodus 19:6 NLT). Just as Israel was to be a kingdom of priests and a holy nation, so today's believers are called "a holy priesthood" (1 Peter 2:5, 9 NLT). God called you so that you could declare His praises before others. Others should see the heavenly Father's character in our lives. All our behavior should be pleasing to God. This book highlights sixteen ways to honor God as you offer your whole life to God.

He used Israel's system of offerings as a way of seeking a right relationship with God. He focused on the five major offerings as the types of spiritual dedication we need overall. They grant us an awareness that we must possess. We are to always confess our sins and ask for forgiveness from God. We need to correct any trespasses or wrongs against our neighbors. God wants us to offer our bodies to Him as complete sacrifices. He directs us to make a concerted effort to do good out of love and concern. Finally, you thank God and trust Him to help you through every concern, problem, need, and want you have. You are learning to put Him first and to enjoy fellowshipping with Jesus. You realize that knowing God secures you eternal life. These offerings to God center around Jesus Christ, our Lord and Savior. At every part of this journey, God is ready to provide the strength and courage you need. God is always ready to support and help you. These same actions are an invitation for God to come into your life more and more.

Above all, giving ourselves to God as complete sacrifices is how we worship and glorify Him. The burnt offering is a type of offering where we present our minds, legs, innards, health, strength, and everything that's left to our loving God. He wants a total sacrifice. He wants us to be full-time believers and soldiers in Christ. There are five areas where we can glorify God. Then all sixteen character behaviors in the book make up your entire life. That's what God desires from you—everything. The bulk of this book is dedicated to specific areas in your life where you can root Jesus more firmly in it. Even as you give God your all, He finds ways for you to be a blessing to others.

In addition, as you do the things mentioned in this book, you are glorifying God. Satan doesn't want you to be so dedicated to God. You are serving God and not yourself. Remember, God is on your side. Then Satan isn't able to deceive you. You are defeating your enemy and winning the battle against him in the spiritual realm. These truths will help you keep the devil under your feet where he belongs. Jesus Christ has the authority and power to deliver us.

Giving yourself totally to God is part of our instructions (Romans 12:1; Luke 10:27). He gives us many ways to sacrifice and worship Him. He accepts what you sacrifice to Him if it is your very best.

Jesus Christ is all these things, and He did all these things while on earth. He gave Himself up for us as a fragrant offering and sacrifice to God.

It is God's love, mercy, and grace that will help you adopt these traits in your life. Remember God loves to see you changing your mind, heart, soul, and strength so that you present yourself totally to Him. He has unimaginable plans for you.

Whatever you need to do, be determined to make those sixteen behaviors apart of your thinking, desire, and enjoyment. Write them down in your Bible. Reread the ways you want to deepen your relationship with God. Take this book with you when wait for appointments and trips or when you just have some free time. Ask God to show you where you need to focus each day. He has unlimited power and the ability to help you walk His way.

You are really a delight to God as He sees you dedicating your time, effort, thoughts, and desires to become the kind of believer He wants. He accepts as you give to him. Now that you know what you can do, enjoy the purpose, peace, and hope God has planned for you. Keep changing and growing toward what Jesus is like. We are His children sealed for an eternal existence and growth with Him (1 Corinthians 1:8–9).

Make these major behaviors habits. Show God you are really dedicated to worshipping Him. God is pleased. God is delighted. God is excited to make good things happen to you. He remembers your sacrifices and accepts your burnt offerings without blemishes (Psalm 20:3 NLT). He accepts what you give to Him, magnifies it, and then gives it back to you.

He gladly accepts the gift of your devotion.

"He will keep you strong to the end, so that you will be blameless on the day of our Lord Jesus Christ. God who has called you into fellowship with his son Jesus Christ our Lord, is faithful" (1 Corinthians 1:8–9).

"May God himself, the God who make everything holy and whole, make you holy and whole, put you together—spirit, soul, and body—and keep you fit for the coming of our Master, Jesus Christ. The one who called you is completely dependable. If he said it, he'll do it!" (1 Thessalonians 5:23–24 The Message).

APPENDIX 1

Jesus is the Center of Our Lives

When you really look at who Jesus is, you realize He has four parts of His life—who He is before coming to earth as a newborn baby, who He is as the divine-human being on earth, who He is after His resurrection, and who He is at His second coming and beyond.

A. The Word Glorified with Father God: Setting the Stage

Along with God, Jesus planned and created the angels and the universe. God had a bold plan to create beings like Him and share eternity with them. The angels were created to serve God and man. The blueprint was drawn up. This must have been a great time of creative design, problem-solving, and dedication. The Father, the Son, and the Holy Spirit were excited about their plan. They worked out every perfect feature for each plant and animal, including us. When the time was right, He spoke the

Word, and it was done (John 1:1–5). The universe and our world were both made at once through Him.

At some time one-third of the angels rebelled with Lucifer. They were defeated by the archangel Michael along with a host of loyal angels. The Word maintains authority and power over the visible and invisible world.

Only God is free from sin. He only is holy, righteous, perfect, and loving. So God purposed to reproduce Himself through humans. First, humankind would be made of flesh and blood. They would be subject to death without the repentance of sin to a loving God. They would have the chance to be born into the divine family begotten by God the Father. God saw humanity could walk this path through the Word, who would become Jesus.

The Word created the universe, the galaxies, and planets. He created animals, plants, and humankind. Then He monitored its condition and growth.

The glory of the Lord rode on a throne powered by four living creatures (Ezekiel 1:26–28). Ezekiel saw in a vision the glory of the Lord departing from the temple above the cherubim (Ezekiel 10:1, 18–19; 11:22–24). The temple was filled with the presence of God.

The Word took the opportunity to preach the gospel to the fallen angels while the world was flooded (1 Peter 3:19–20 NASB).

God selected His chosen nation, Israel, to bring about the needed milestones in history. He called and tested Abraham. Then God passed the Promised Land to Isaac and Jacob. He led Moses and Israel out of slavery. His people were formed for His glory. He called Israel to be a light and witness to the nations around it. He called and guided the right kings and prophets. He foretold what was going to happen and then brought it to pass. He showed that those who believe that God is the LORD will be blessed. God confirmed there is no God besides Him (Isaiah 44:6–8; 43:10–13 NASB). We are Abraham's seed and heirs to the promise of eternal life. This is the Israel connection.

God watches and gets involved in the affairs of humanity and nations. God can do whatever He wants to do with nations and kingdoms (Jeremiah 18:5–10 NKJV). He searches the hearts and minds of people in order to know their intents. God was involved with key prophets, kings, leaders, and common people.

The scriptures were inspired by God. It is useful for teaching, rebuking, correcting, and training in righteousness (2 Timothy 3:16–17 NLT). He wants to prepare and equip us to do every good work. Jesus is the revelator of Revelation, all prophecy, and the entire Bible. He does this by the Holy Spirit.

The Word became the High Priest to Abraham and accepted tithes from him. The Word was Melchizedek, king of Salem (king of peace) and priest of God, the Most High. He was without father or mother, without genealogy, without beginning of days or end of life. As the Son of God, he remains a priest forever. Of course, Jesus was of the order of Melchizedek (Hebrews 7:1–3, 13–17).

Before the world was made, the Word volunteered to come out of a divine nature and go into a human. He would shed His blood for humankind. The Word is perfect in character, thoughts, ways, and love. This set the stage for everything God wanted to do for humanity.

The Word has become the centerpiece for the plan of salvation for humankind. He would also be the fulfillment of Israel's offerings and festivals. He was set to be first among the firstfruits for eternal life. He becomes the only way we humans can become children of God.

We will be called and saved for Father God's own purpose and grace. This grace was given us in Christ Jesus before the beginning of time (2 Timothy 1:9 NLT). Grace as a gift was God's plan from the beginning. God knew that His mercy, forgiveness, and grace would produce the loving way.

We don't know everything that the Word did before coming to earth as a human. However, He was a part of all the efforts mentioned previously in some way.

B. Jesus the Divine-Human Being on Earth

Jesus is sent by the Father to do His will, expand our understanding of God, obey in every way, glorify the Father, and show others He is a loving and forgiving God.

Let's look at some of the things Jesus Christ did while on earth. He fulfilled all of the work the Father gave Him to do.

1. Jesus did/does a number of things that shows He is the Messiah.

He did many miracles out of love and concern.

He taught lessons to common people, rich and poor, sinners, women, Jews and Gentiles, the disabled, and the Pharisees with authority. He always told them the truth. Jesus pointed to the Kingdom of God.

He used life-teaching parables and real-life situations to make His points.

He knew and used the scriptures rightly and better than any person before Him.

He prepared us for a place in His Kingdom. He and the Spirit make sure we get the experiences we need to fulfill our chosen purpose and position. We are given specific gifts and talents (John 14:2–3; 17:6, 9 NKJV).

He sends the Holy Spirit to be our teacher, advocate, and counselor (John 14:26; 16:13–14 NKJV).

He keeps creation running by holding things together (Colossians 1:15–17; Ephesians 1:10; John 2:32–35 NKJV).

Since Jesus shared what He knows about the Father, He wants us also to share things about Him.

Jesus wants us to know and thus love Father God.

He protects us from the evil one by His authority (John 17:5 NJKV).

Jesus commissioned His church to preach and publish the gospel to all the world (Mark 13:10). Believers today also have that same commission. We can act as witnesses for God.

2. Jesus became the source and means of everything we hold dear.

Our sins are forgiven because of Jesus's death (Romans 6:8–11; 10:9).

He is the author and finisher of our faith (Hebrews 12:2).

Grace and mercy is given because of Jesus's death and resurrection (Ephesians 2:4–5).

You will please Father only through Him (Hebrews 13:4).

He is the bread of life. We learn and live in the truth (John 6:27, 35).

He is the only way to salvation (John 14:6–7).

He is our true light and encourages us to live in His light (1 John 1:9–11; 8:12).

As the true shepherd, He is our source of guidance, protection, and help (John 10:11–15).

We are given grace in Christ before time began (2 Timothy 1:9).

We might become the righteousness of God through Jesus (2 Corinthians 5:21).

We have the means to understand how Jesus is the reality of both the offerings and the many festivals.

Our personal difficulties are solved because He is always with us and in us.

He is our means for growing to maturity (Ephesians 4:12–13, 15).

Your peace, joy, and hope comes through Jesus (Romans 15:13).

We are freed from sin and death because of Jesus (Romans 6:18).

Our relationship with the Father is restored and is growing (John 17:25).

Our Father loves us since we love Jesus (John 14:23).

We love others because Jesus shows us how in His examples.

As head of the church, Jesus give us the means to become a holy temple where God lives. (Ephesians 2:19–22).

We become new creatures by Him (2 Corinthians 5:17–18).

As our High Priest, He gives us confidence to approach the Father in prayer (Hebrews 7:15–17).

We are being transformed from lowly bodies to be like Jesus Christ's glorious body (Philippians 3:21).

Since Jesus does the Father's will, we have the desire and hope to do this as well.

3. Jesus pointed to many things that confirm His divine nature.

He foretold the signs for the end times (Matthew 24).

He was sent by the Father (John 10:33–39).

He forgives sin (Ephesians 1:7).

Jesus is our Lord and Savior (John 9:35–41).

The Holy Spirit is to further teach us how to be like Jesus Christ (John 16:13–14).

He will be fully glorified and sit at the right hand of the Father (Colossians 3:1–4).

We will serve Jesus forever (Ephesians 2:6–7).

He is returning to earth as the Son of God (1 Thessalonians 4:15–17).

He will resurrect those who belong to Him (John 17:1–2).

He prophesied that He will be the world's coming King and Lord over nations. We will rule with Him (Matthew 24:30–31).

He dwells in us through the Spirit (Romans 8:9–11).

He predicted the chaotic conditions of today's world. He also foretold the outcome of it all.

Father God speaks to us by His Son, Jesus (Hebrews 1:2–3).

Jesus drives out impure spirits by His authority (Luke 4:33–36).

His life as a perfect divine-human being qualified Him to die once for all humankind—past, present, and the future. Thus, Jesus died for us gladly, knowing His part in the plan.

C. Reglorified Son of God

Jesus was resurrected by the Father. He ascended to the Father in heaven (John 20:17; Colossians 3:1–4).

Jesus was given the glory, authority, and power He had before the creation of the world (John 17:1–5, 24).

Jesus Christ is still doing all the things listed previously.

Jesus defeated death and brought life and immortality by the gospel (2 Timothy 1:10).

He is actively preparing a place for us in His kingdom.

He guides His church and encourages us to be ready for His second coming (Luke 21:36).

He keeps creation working smoothly (Colossians 1:16–18).

He intercedes for us as a mediator of the new covenant (Hebrews 7:25; 8:6).

He is opening minds and hearts for more people to come to Him and be saved.

He opens the seven seals to fulfill the prophecy for the end time (Revelation 1:1–2, 17b).

D. The King of Kings and Lord of Lords

Jesus will return as King of Kings and Lord of Lords to save humans from themselves (Daniel 2:44; Revelation 11:15). He will call the children the Father gave Him to eternal life. He will destroy the vast armies gathering to destroy Israel. Jerusalem is sacred to God. The glorified saints will be with Him forever. We will be priests of God and Christ. He will set up His kingdom based on love. Many people will receive the truth and be saved. The government of God will be restored completely without Satan's presence and influence for one thousand years. It will be a beautiful world. The human heart is humbled and converted. Those same people will be given the very nature of God. The final judgment will be given by Jesus. He knows those who desire and hunger for grace. He knows the people who are healed, saved and filled with the Holy Spirit. He is merciful, loving, and righteous. When everything is conquered under the rule and authority of the Son of God, He will give it back to Father God.

The holy city, Jerusalem, will be brought down from heaven by the Father. A new earth will also be formed. Earth will become the center of the universe. The Father and Jesus Christ will come to earth to be our God, and we will be His people. God is the source of light and truth to the world.

After all have received their inheritance and mission, the children of God will be sent out into the galaxies of the universe. Planets will be made ready to sustain life. Creation is waiting on the children of God to renew it and complete it (Romans 8:19–22). The planets will be developed for human-life through the guidance of Christ God and Father God. Along with the loyal angels, we will guide the righteous character development of countless humans. They shall also become the sons and heirs of the sovereign God and members of the great God family. The kingdom of God will forever expand into the universe.

There are several heart felt chilling songs in the Handel's Messiah collection that gives reasons to rejoice and be thankful for what Jesus was, is, and forever be. He did everything He needed to do. He came as a child and becomes Wonderful, Counselor, and King of Kings of the earth ("Unto Us a Child is Born"). Our Lord is our redeemer ("I Know My Redeemer Lives"). The Lamb of God becomes our Savior ("Behold the Lamb of God") The trumpet will announce Jesus' return to earth ("The Trumpet Shall Sound"). The King will defeat any nation that refuse to change ("Thou Shall Break Them"). We will rejoice at Jesus's coming to bring His new government ("The Hallelujah Chorus ").

"Since then, you have been raised with Christ, set your hearts on things above, where Christ is, seated at the right hand of God. Set your minds on things above, not on earthly things. For you died, and your life is now hidden with Christ in God. When Christ, who is your life, appears, then you also will appear with him in glory" (Colossians 3:1–4).

Songs to Praise and Thank God

Many of these tracks can be found on YouTube if you would like to hear people actually singing these songs.

Offer Our Sacrifice

"Every Time that We Are Gathered" by Denise Graves
"We Are an Offering" by Dwight Liles
"I Smile" by Kirk Franklin
"I Will Celebrate" by Rita Baloche

Fellowship Offering

"No Higher Calling" by Larry LeBlanc and Greg Guilley
"I Need You" by Donnie McClurkin
Christ in Us Be Glorified" by Morris Chapman

Know Jesus Better

"Knowing You" by Graham Kendrick
"Draw Me into Your Presence" by Teresa Muller
"Break Every Chain" by Tasha Cobbs
"He Knows My Name" by Tommy Walker
"Above All" by Lenny LeBlanc
"He Is Able" by Rory Noland/Grey Ferguson
"Never Have to Be Alone" by Ce Ce Winans

Sing to God

"I Can Only Imagine" by Tamela Mann
"There'll Always Be" by Tommy Walker
"Shout to the Lord" by Darlene Zschech
"Lord, I Lift Your Name on High" by Rick Founds
"Jesus Is Love" by Lionel Richie

Love of God

"Baptize Us with Your Love" by Kelly Willard
"For the Love of the People" by The Clark Sisters
"The Battle Is Not Yours" by Yolanda Adams

Praise God

"We Bring the Sacrifice of Praise" by Kirk Dearman
"You are Worthy of Praise" by David Ruis
"Praise Him in Advance" by Marvin Sapp
"Indescribable" by Kierra Sneard

Thank God

"Undivided Heart" by Dan Marks

Conclusion

"Take This Life" by Jachin Mullen
"This Is Your House" by Don Moen
"Withholding Nothing" by William McDowell
"I Give Myself Away" by William McDowell
"Awesome" by Charles Jenkins

BIBLIOGRAPHY

Atkins, Donald, and Charles Roesel. *Meeting Needs—Sharing Christ.* Nashville: LifeWay Press, 1995.

Kay, David, and B. J Lawson. *Loving God and Others.* Colorado Springs, CO: WaterBrook Press, 2009.

Blackaby, H. Richard, and Claude King. *Experiencing God.* Nashville: LifeWay Press, 2011.

Booze, Mike. *John 17:1–8: Glory to God!* Shreveport, LA. Faith Community, 2010.

Booze, Mike. *Acts 9:32–43: Your Efforts Count.* Shreveport, LA: Faith Community, 2012.

Booze, Mike. *Motivation: Why Be Submissive to Government Authority.* Shreveport, LA: Faith Community. 2015.

Booze, Mike. *Acts 11:19–26: Everyone's Commission!* Shreveport, LA. Faith Community Shreveport.

Booze, Mike. *The Ministry of All Believers.* Shreveport, LA: Faith Community. Accessed on April 1, 2016, www.graceinternet.org.

Booze, Mike. *The Breakfast of Champions: Habit of Thanksgiving.* Shreveport, LA: Faith Community, 2016, www.graceinternet.org.

Booze, Mike. *Who Is the Greatest in the Kingdom.* Shreveport, LA: Faith Community, 2017.

Bradford, Bill. *God the Father Series*. Shreveport, LA: Worldwide Church of God, 1983.

Deffinbaugh, Bob. "From Series Leviticus: Sacrifice and Sanctification Series: The Law of Burnt Offerings." Accessed on May 18, 2014. http:/ series/leviticus-sacrifice-and-sanctification/2-law-of-burnt-offerings.

Draper, Richard. "Sacrifices and Offerings." Accessed June 6, 2013. http://lds/ ensign/1980/og/Sacrifices-and-Offerings-foreshadowings-of-christ?!=eng.

Duke, Russell. "Several Functions of Priest." December 14, 1991.

Duke, Russell. "Duties and Rules of a Priest Today." December 21, 1991.

George, Jim. *The 50 Most Important Teachings of the Bible*. Colorado Springs, CO: WaterBrook Press, 2009.

Got Questions Ministries, 2002–2010. "Why Did God Require Animal Sacrifices in the Old Testament." Accessed on July 20, 2010. www. gotquestions.org/aniamal-sacrifices.html.

Got Questions Ministries, 2002–2018. "What Is a Sin Offering?" Accessed on July 21, 2016. http://gotquestions.org/sin-offering.html.

Hunt, Mical. Agape Bible Study. "The Levitical Sacrifices & Offerings of the Sinai Covenant." Accessed on July 25, 2010. http://agapebiblestudy. com/charts/Levitcal%20Sacrifices%20and%20Offerings.

Holman Bible Dictionaries. "Sacrifice and Offerings." Accessed on June 6, 2013. http:/www.studylight.org/dictionaries/hbd/S/Sacrifice-andofferings.html.

Jakes, T. D. *When Power Meets Potential: Unlocking God's Purpose in Your Life*. Shipensburg, PA: Destiny Image Publishers, Inc., 2014.

Junkovich, Brad. *Gut Check*. Bossier, LA. First Bossier, 2017.

Junkovich, Brad. *Relationship Reset with God: Summer 2017 Series*. Bossier, LA: First Bossier, 2017.

Kaufiln, Bob. *The Three R's: Why Christians Sing*. March 20, 2011.

Kendrick, Stephen and Alex. *The Battle Plan for Prayer*. Nashville: B & H Publishing Group, 2015.

McMillian, Elton. "The Five Levitical Offerings: Trespass Offering." Accessed on September 6, 2016. http://www.bibleteachingonline101. net/Trespass-offering_html.

McMillian, Elton. "The Five Levitical Offerings: Burnt Offering." Accessed on September 6, 2016. http://www.bibleteachingonline101. net/Burnt-offering.html.

Myer, Joyce. *Eight Ways to Keep the Devil Under Your Feet*. New York: FaithWords, Hachette Book Group, 2006.

Myer, Joyce. *Power Thoughts*. New York: FaithWords, Hachette Book Group, 2010.

Myer, Joyce. *Unshakable Trust*. New York: FaithWords, Hachette Book Group, 2017.

Laurie, Greg. *Tell Someone: You Can Share the Good News*. Nashville: LifeWay Press, 2016.

Montgomery, John. "Keeping the Offering Fire Constantly Burning." Radio 88.1 FM. Broadcast on August 1, 2017.

Moore, Beth. *Discovering God's Purpose for Your Life*. Addison, TX: Dunham Books Addison, 2005.

Moore, Cedric. "Live a Godly Life in spite of Living in an Ungodly World". Shreveport, LA: Faith Community, April 19,2015.

Moore, Cedric. "Living Spiritual Sacrifice". Shreveport, LA: Faith Community, June 25, 2017.

Moore, John. "Obedience". Shreveport, LA: Faith Community, October 16,2016.

Moore, John. "Tell the Truth". Shreveport, LA: Faith Community, May 28, 2017.

Nadler, Sam. *Messiah in the Feast of Israel*. Word of Messiah Ministries, 2010.

Realtime.net. "Levitical Sacrifices and Offerings." Accessed on June 6, 2013. http://www.realtime.net/~wdoud/levitsac.html.

Rich, Tracey. "Judaism 101: Qorbanot: Sacrifices and Offerings." Accessed on September 6, 2016. http://www.jewfaq.org/qorbanot.htm.

Stanley, Charles. "Convicted about Eternal Security." Intouch Ministries. FETV 6:00 ct. Broadcast on April 2, 2017.

Stanley, Charles. *Handle with Care*. ".Colorado Springs, CO: David C. Cook, 2011.

Stanley, Charles. "Christ's Blood Essential for Salvation." From Pastor's Heart Letter in February 2017. Monthly letter to subscribers.

Stanley, Charles. "Servanthood." From Pastor's Heart Letter in June 2017. Monthly letter to subscribers.

Stanley, Charles. "Be Thankful." From Pastor's Heart Letter in November 2017. Monthly letter to subscribers.

Tam, Stephen. "The Five Offerings in the Old Testament." Accessed on July 26, 2010. http://www.telus.net/public/kstam/en/tabernacle/details/offerings.htm.

Walter, Elwell A. "Offerings and Sacrifice." *Baker's Evangelical Dictionary of Biblical Theology.* Accessed on June 6, 2013. http://www.biblestudytools.com/dictionaries/bakers-evangelical-dictionary/offerings-and-sacrifices.hml.

Warren, Rick. "The Good Samaritan in the Bible." Daily Hope Devotion. July 2017.

Woodsel, Andrew. "Should We Trust Our Governing Authorities?" August 10, 2017.

Young, William. *The Shack.* Newbury Park, CA: Windblown Media, FaithWords, Hoddler & Stoughton, 2007.

Printed in the United States
By Bookmasters